Battle Rattle

THE STUFF A SOLDIER CARRIES

HANS HALBERSTADT

ZENITH PRESS

JUN 0 1 2007

DEDICATION

For Mike Noell, with a salute for his pioneering role in getting better warfighter gear to the warfighters.

First published in 2006 by MBI Publishing Company LLC and Zenith Press, an imprint of MBI Publishing Company, Galtier Plaza, Suite 200, 380 Jackson Street, St Paul, MN, 55101-3885 USA

The information in this book is true and complete to the best of our knowledge. All recommendations are made without any guarantee on the part of the author or Publisher, who also disclaim any liability incurred in connection with the use of this data or specific details.

We recognize that some words, model names and designations, for example, mentioned herein are the Property of the trademark holder. We use them for identification purposes only. This is not an official publication.

Zenith Press books are also available at discounts in bulk quantity for industrial or sales-promotional use. For details write to Special Sales Manager at MBI Wholesalers & Distributors, Galtier Plaza, Suite 200, 380 Jackson Street, St Paul, MN, 55101-3885 USA.

ISBN-13: 978-0-7603-2622-0
ISBN-10: 0-7603-2622-3

Editor: Scott Pearson and Steve Gansen
Designer: LeAnn Kuhlmann

Printed in China

Library of Congress Cataloging-in-Publication Data

Halberstadt, Hans.
 Battle rattle : the stuff a soldier carries / Hans Halberstadt.
    p. cm.
  ISBN-13: 978-0-7603-2622-0 (plc)
  ISBN-10: 0-7603-2622-3 (plc)
  1. United States—Armed Forces—Equipment.
  2. Soldiers—United States. I. Title.
  UC463.H35 2006
  355.80973—dc22

                          2006019828

ABOUT THE AUTHOR

Hans Halberstadt has authored and co-authored more than fifty books, mostly on military subjects, especially U.S. special operations forces, armor, and artillery. Halberstadt served in the U.S. Army as a helicopter door gunner in Vietnam. He and his wife, April, live in San Jose, California.

On the cover: With helmet-mounted night-vision goggles, binoculars, radio with H250 handset, CamelBak hydration system, and plenty of ammo, this warfighter carries a lot of stuff.

On the frontispiece: RECON marines carry some of the heaviest rucks in the warfighting business.

On the title pages: When combined with radio communications, a smoke grenade can verify the identity of a ground force.

On the back cover:
(top left) A soldier of the 2nd Battalion, 8th Infantry Regiment, 4th Infantry Division, carries everything but the kitchen sink.

(top right) This SEAL's chest rig has all the ammo he wants—where he wants it.

(bottom right) A sampling of one infantryman's ruck, from underwear to Gore-Tex jacket.

CONTENTS

Foreword

A Revolution in Soldier Systems
by Eric Graves

Eric Graves is one of the senior "gear gurus" of the U.S. armed forces. His experience with warfighter equipment began as a soldier, who, like every soldier twenty years ago, used the M1967 series of equipment. Since then he has served with special operations forces (SOF) that had special requirements and the budgets to support them. These assignments put Graves on the ground floor of the modern revolution in the development of soldier systems and combat equipment. He has helped design and acquire some of the new equipment, and he has seen the revolution from the perspective of a designer as well as a user.

Like many boys, I liked playing soldier as a kid and, as I always had lots of war-surplus military gear around the house, playing army became pretty realistic. I loved digging through newly arrived lots at the surplus store, poring over ads in *Shotgun News*, and making regular pilgrimages to local gun shows. Over time my collection grew. Later, I joined the army, and I had some great jobs that allowed me to experiment with my gear and try out new things.

While in Germany during the 1980s, I began to use kit manufactured by Arktis and Special Air Sea Services in England. These British companies were light-years ahead of the United States in the development of commercially viable soldier-systems equipment. I think it was because the standard-issue British kit had become so outdated and Britain's fairly recent experience in the Falkland Islands had focused the British "Tommy" on real warfighting.

Back then, getting each issue of the British magazine *Combat and Survival* was like receiving a new Sears Christmas Wishbook. I was not the only one excited about it; many of my fellow unit members also sported Arktis chest rigs in the field. About the same time, I also started adapting civilian products for military use. Commercial camping gear was warmer and weighed less than our issue gear. The problems with recreational equipment for military use were cost, durability, and color schemes, but we overcame those issues. Modifying kit became a necessity based on our mission. I would paint, dye, or otherwise modify everything from sleeping pads to backpacks. Other guys in my company's barracks were dyeing civilian sleeping bags dark colors so often that when you used the washing machines you took a risk your whites would come out gray.

Eventually, I developed a reputation for finding the good stuff, and later in my career, adapting new products for military use became part of my duties. I had become a true gear guru.

So what are soldier systems? Affectionately known as "battle rattle," "TA-50," 782, "deuce gear," kit, or just plain old gear, they are most accurately described as items that the soldier eats, wears, or carries in order to accomplish his mission.

I have always found it ironic that the most important weapon on the battlefield—the fighter—has often been given the least attention. A warfighter's gear tends to be fairly inexpensive compared to aircraft, tanks, and other systems, and it can greatly improve the living conditions (and save the life) of soldiers or Marines. But despite the relatively low cost, it seems as though only armies in the West have bothered to provide quality individual equipment to their personnel, and some of those in only the last few years, as governments have done away with conscription and moved toward professional armies. Combat boots are far from sexy, and you don't build a recruiting commercial around them. What's more, boot manufacturers aren't going to make large contributions to a politician's campaign fund. But nothing will put a smile on a grunt's face like a good pair of boots.

The Recent Revolution in Soldier Systems

As the Cold War wound down in the late 1990s, the idea of a revolution in military affairs began to emerge. The concept was going to transform the U.S. military into a high-tech, computerized, network-centric force that would fight smarter instead of harder. The concept was predicated on outthinking the enemy and winning a war without committing U.S. ground forces. But the types of enemies the U.S. military began to encounter became stumbling blocks to implementation. Ultimately, the new foe could only be defeated with one weapon, the American soldier.

However, the environment that sparked the idea of the military-affairs revolution also made a true soldier-systems revolution possible. First, gear innovation shifted from the government using taxpayers' dollars to private industry using private funds. Second, the U.S. military began to change the way it spent its money. The international merchant purchase authorization card (IMPAC) made it possible for a unit-level supply officer to purchase goods and services directly from commercial sources.

Congress had enacted the Berry Amendment years before as a means of protecting the domestic textile industry for times of war. This amendment requires that the Department of Defense procure textile goods that are manufactured within the United States from U.S.-made materials. But a loophole for "micropurchases" below $100,000 allows units to buy foreign products. This loophole is often used by small units, such as special-operations forces (SOF), to get around the restriction and get the best gear available for combat. The soldier was no longer stuck with equipment built to government specifications from the lowest bidder, and the term "government issue" has been set on its ear.

The third and most critical piece of this soldier-systems revolution was the patenting of the pouch attachment ladder system (PALS) by Natick Soldier Systems Center, the U.S. Army and Marine Corps' research facility for gear. This basket weave–like system is used to attach pouches and other accessories to "platforms" such as armor vests, chest rigs, and packs. It is amazing that something that simple could have such a deep impact on the individual soldier, but PALS put soldiers in control of their load by giving them the flexibility to tailor the amount and configuration of their individual equipment. When a new load-bearing system is fielded, the unit simply purchases new PALS-compatible pouches from a variety of vendors.

Since the patent was issued, controversy has raged over who actually developed this technology. Many desire credit for its design because PALS enabled modular lightweight load carrying equipment (MOLLE)—the current U.S. load-carrying system of platforms and pouches—to happen.

Soldier Systems Development

From the War of Independence to the late 1990s, the development of soldier systems was evolutionary in nature—a series of incremental changes. Leather was replaced with webbing, a new color might emerge, or the adoption of a new rifle might force a change in the size of a cartridge box, but overall, what the warfighters carried and what it weighed changed little. For example, the ancient shelter half tent retained the same size and shape from the Civil War into the twenty-first century and has only recently been replaced.

To illustrate what I mean by evolutionary development—and demonstrate how revolutionary PALS is—a history lesson is in order.

Load-bearing vests (LBVs) can be found toward the end of World War I, when a chest rig was developed to carry eleven hand grenades for the great offensive of 1919 that never occurred. In World War II, the "Battle Jerkin" was issued to U.S. Rangers during the Normandy invasion. Various experimental and indigenous assault vests were tested in Vietnam, but none ever found general issue.

Load-bearing vests—whether M1910 webbing, M1956, M1967, or all-purpose lightweight individual carrying equipment (ALICE)—all featured essentially static designs. While a pouch could be moved around on a pistol belt via a 1910 belt hanger or an ALICE clip, there was very little flexibility. For example, the 40mm grenade-launcher load required a separate vest, which was worn over the standard load-carrying systems. Even though the tactical load-bearing vest was issued in the early 1990s, it took several years for a grenadier version of that vest to be introduced.

The first time we see what appears to be an issue modular vest was during the invasion of Grenada. Members of the 75th Ranger Regiment used an olive-drab (OD) version of Elevated Urban Operation's quick-reaction vest. It used a Velcro-and-snap combination to hold the pouches onto the vest. In the mid-1980s, several commercial designs were available for private purchase, but they mainly saw use with special-operations forces.

Since the late 1970s, the U.S. Marine Corps has been seeking to do away with the cartridge or pistol belt. It developed and tested a nonmodular LBV that put all of the Marine's required items on the body of the vest. This same attribute was later featured in the first generation of MOLLE. The design was refined and issued to the 9th Infantry Division high-technology test bed in the mid-1980s. Later, it served as the genesis for the tactical load bearing vest portion of the individual integrated fighting system (IIFS). The IIFS consisted of a tactical LBV, a field pack large internal frame (FPLIF) rucksack, an individual multipurpose shelter (IMPS), and a sleep system. Early IIFS systems were fielded to SOFs like the SEALs and Green Berets as well as the 7th and 10th Light Divisions.

The tactical LBV was modified in 1994, and refinements were made based on operational use. The angle of the magazine pouches was changed, and the Cordura body of the vest was replaced with mesh. This new version was dubbed the "enhanced tactical LBV" and remained standard issue until replaced with the MOLLE system right after 2000. (I credit former Commandant of the Marine Corps General Charles C. Krulak with revamping the 782 gear or individual equipment. During his tenure, he made the individual Marine his number-one priority, and many new systems were developed, including the interceptor body armor [IBA] that has saved so many lives in Iraq.)

With MOLLE, the Marine Corps insisted on an integrated cartridge and rucksack load-bearing waist belt. The belt was meant to unclutter the Marine's waist, but its infamous ball-and-socket design was prone to breakage and difficult to use. This led to the corps' dissatisfaction with MOLLE, and a short-notice program for a commercial replacement system was launched. Ultimately, a pack designed by the Canadian outdoor company ARC'TERYX was adopted as the improved load-bearing equipment (ILBE) rucksack. (It was manufactured in Puerto Rico

by Propper in order to accommodate the Berry Amendment.)

The U.S. Army learned from the Marine Corps' first experience with MOLLE. It not only replaced the ball-and-socket frame with a fixed waist belt, but also put together training teams to teach small-unit leaders how to properly configure and use MOLLE. During the initial Marine Corps experiments, young Marines were confused with the large bag of MOLLE pouches and components; the army provided a similar bag of new gear to soldiers, but also provided instructors to help them put it all together properly.

As of this writing in 2006, we have seen at least three distinct generations of MOLLE, but it's really a living system that is constantly being refined. A MOLLE system issued today looks radically different from one issued as little as two years ago. Not only has the camouflage pattern changed from woodland to three-color desert to universal-camouflage pattern, but the size of the rucksack has also changed. The frame is more durable, and the quantity and types of pouches are different. Natick Soldier Systems Center's experimental load-carrying facility constantly interacts with the army's operational forces and modifies current MOLLE components or develops entirely new ones based on warfighter reports and suggestions from the field.

Commercial pouches and packs featuring PALS or PALS-compatible attachment systems have been offered by dozens of manufacturers, large and small. A soldier can find a pouch for anything, and if it doesn't exist, a call to one of several custom manufacturers, like RecceGear, will yield a final product in a matter of days. Companies like Spec-Ops and Tactical Tailor churn out low-cost, durable pouches and often serve as a soldier's first foray into commercial equipment. Many soldiers soon supplement these pouches with more expensive designs. Because the MOLLE system is so flexible, there is rarely a complaint from the chain of command, so long as the equipment blends in.

Special Operations: The Traditional Testing Ground

Whether carbines or radios, rucksacks or underwear, whatever America's special-operations forces issue to their operators will eventually find its way to the general-purpose forces. And for good reason—Special Operations Command (SOCOM) controls its own budget and endeavors to provide the best equipment it can find for its personnel. SOCOM fields its systems quickly and subjects them to the most demanding conditions on earth. By following SOCOM's lead, other U.S. service branches, like the army, can save research-and-development dollars and field equipment more quickly.

For example, the M4 carbine, first issued to SOCOM, now has almost replaced the M16A2 in the army, due to its many virtues in the cramped urban environment of Iraq. The army also adopted many components of the SOPMOD (special-operations peculiar modification) kit with Picatinny M1913 rails, which enabled many sights and sighting attachments to be clipped onto the rifle or carbine and thus improve the weapon's functionality.

When the army wanted to update its cold-weather issue, it initially took a page from the SOF's personal equipment advanced requirements (SPEAR) lightweight environmental-protection (LEP) undergarments. Eventually they eyed a simplified version of LEP's replacement, the protective combat uniform issued to SEALs.

In 2003, the Marine Corps adopted its own distinct camouflage patterns. The army and air force both quickly followed suit, and now even the navy is preparing to issue its own digital-pattern uniform. Each service has gone its own way and in some cases stepped on each other's toes while getting in line at the few U.S. mills that can adequately print digital fabrics. Not only are uniform designs and patterns different, but everything from T-shirts to caps to boots is also different. Regardless of service, soldiers want to be draped from head to toe in their team's colors. The desire to be distinct has driven up the cost of uniforms and will ultimately spill over into other soldier-system gear.

What Does the Future Hold?

We are beginning to see the emergence of what I call hybrid systems. Hybrids combine traditional fixed pockets with the flexibility of PALS panels. On any given platform, whether an assault vest or rucksack, there are certain pockets you are always going to use, and you will always want them in the same place. This is particularly true of ammunition pockets for which muscle memory is critical. On the other hand, you may not always use the same type of radio, or for that matter a radio at all, so the PALS panel offers the ability to tailor the load. The pendulum has swung so far in favor of modularity that entire rucksacks are covered from top to bottom in a latticework of PALS webbing. Hybrid systems offer lower cost as well as weight savings by eliminating extraneous PALS webbing. Instead, fixed pouches are sewn directly to the platform; in some cases neither pocket nor PALS webbing will adorn the unused space.

Not only will kit design change, but how it is actually constructed will change as well. The outdoor industry has been using welded-seam technology in clothing for years, and companies are beginning to adapt this technology to the production of packs. ARC'TERYX has designed a civilian pack made from two pieces of fabric that are welded together with urethane. Every stitch in a piece of fabric weakens it, so the ability to use fewer pieces of material and to hold them together in new ways strengthens the final product.

Many aftermarket manufacturers build completely bombproof gear, made from several layers of 1000D Cordura (and in some cases even scuba-belt webbing), but the gear is heavy even before the soldier begins to fill the kit with mission-essential equipment. Some are beginning to question just how durable is durable enough and if newer, high-tenacity fabrics like 725D can replace the 1000D Cordura. If commercial manufacturers can find the right balance between weight and durability, the soldier will be the real winner.

If soldiers continue to supplement issue gear with commercial products from a variety of manufacturers, the job of combat developers becomes more difficult. They will often find themselves acting as integrators and serving as advocates to industry, convincing companies to shave as much weight as possible, foster innovation, and, as we see the increased requirement for electronic integration in our soldier systems, designate commercial standards for manufacturing. The load-bearing system will soon serve as the soldier's serial bus; in the future a soldier will carry a small computer and his various electronics will connect to that computer to enhance his situational awareness. Essentially every soldier on the battlefield will become a sensor, and the data he passively collects as he conducts his mission will be merged at headquarters with other data into a holistic view of the battlespace to be used by decision makers and trigger pullers alike. Companies like Suunto manufacture wrist-top computers, which constantly collect Global Positioning System (GPS), physiological, and meteorological data. The key is to develop a way to upload that data from the soldier, through his onboard communications backbone, and into the hands of leaders—and industry must be prepared for this next step.

The biggest downside to the Berry Amendment is that the U.S. textile industry is, for the most part, not innovative. You can blame globalization, but the U.S. textile industry exists for profit, and the margins are much better overseas. New materials, and the development of the special processes required to manufacture them, are concentrated outside the United States. Since such foreign-made gear is not Berry compliant, products that use these latest manufacturing techniques cannot become issue items. Although many manufacturers continue to operate in the United States and turn a profit, certain advanced manufacturing processes are unavailable to them. We are caught in somewhat of a catch-22. Manufacturers will not invest in new materials or machinery because government specs don't call for them, and the government won't insist on these advancements because they aren't already available in the marketplace. Hopefully, someone will consider all of the variables and assume the risk of investing in new machinery. If companies can manufacture domestically and still turn a profit despite a serious investment in new infrastructure, their competitors will be forced to follow suit in order to remain viable.

However, many companies realize that the margins are very tight for government contracts, so they sell their products either through direct-marketing to units and soldiers or via wholesalers, whose products are marketed by military outfitters such as Diamondback Tactical, Brigade Quartermaster, or U.S. Cavalry.

While Britain has in the past been a source of innovative equipment, British equipment development has followed a more evolutionary path than the United States. There has been no PALS revolution in Great Britain. The British military completely replaced its outdated kit with Soldier 95 items, and its commercial soldier-systems market almost dried up. While there remains a market for nonissue kit in England, thanks mainly

to current combat operations, the equipment you see for sale today has changed little in the last twenty years. Several other European countries are experimenting with versions of PALS. Germany has a version of PALS that features both vertical and horizontal webbing. But surprisingly, the idea of a truly modular approach hasn't caught on in Europe.

New isn't always better. It seems like old ideas constantly resurface, and some classics have remained favorites. The classic five-button sweater and watch caps have only recently been replaced with synthetics, but due to renewed concerns about flash burns, we may see a return to clothing made from natural fibers. The Marine Corps recently banned the use of synthetic undergarments like Under Armor to help mitigate flash burns. The venerable poncho liner, or woobie, has yet to be seriously replaced. Several companies have attempted to market improved Ranger blankets with high-tech insulation, but prices have been prohibitive, and they lack the compression of the original poncho liner.

Even with the change in operational environments we now see, the principles of camouflage remain the same. Soldiers want to blend in with their environment. Everyone remembers seeing SOF operators early in Operation Enduring Freedom wearing civilian clothing so as to better blend in with their Northern Alliance allies. In the future we may well see the emergence of "civvy-flage," commercial clothing with military utility.

Both SOF and general-purpose forces like cold-weather gear from Patagonia and Mountain Hardware, boots from a gamut of manufacturers, and many other commercial items. Purpose-built clothing and equipment already exists from 5.11, Woolrich, and CamelBak, but I see even more developments. BlackHawk Products Group has taken the commercial military market by storm with an entire array of equipment and continues to expand its line as needs change.

SOF requirements will continue to drive innovation for soldier systems. Former niche companies, like Paraclete, Eagle Industries, and London Bridge Trading Company, have now come into prominence, as the average soldier wants to use the same equipment as the heavy hitters. Much like sports fans want to use the same glove as their favorite baseball star, members of the Big Green want to use the gear that has proven valuable to SOF. And there is no reason a soldier in the 3rd Infantry Division deserves any less protection than a member of a Special Forces Operational Detachment Alpha (ODA). Both face the same threats. I could never hope to mention every company that is doing marvelous things in this multifaceted industry.

While the greater revolution in military affairs moves slowly, the revolution in soldier systems has been an unmitigated success. My hat is off to the services' acquisition communities for their leadership and their partnering with industry.

The American soldier has never been so well equipped.

Acknowledgments

This book has been evolving for many years and contains the combined wisdom and experience of many Marines, soldiers, and warfighters from the U.S. Coast Guard, U.S. Navy, U.S. Air Force, and members of the British army. Much of this book's information is based on the efforts of people and organizations in the private sector, working on their own initiative, to provide high-quality equipment to warfighters in the armed forces, and much of the book's information comes from industry sources as well as uniformed personnel.

I would be badly remiss, however, if I failed to salute the following individuals, each of whom has made a major contribution to this book: Stephen "Chief" Bronson, USN Boat Guy, Retired; Steve Dondero, Eye Safety Systems (ESS); Dan Freeman, Wiley X; Sgt. Maj. Glenn, S3 Sergeant Major, 4th Brigade, 25th Infantry Division (Airborne); Maj. Charles Greene, S3, 4th Brigade, 25th Infantry Division; Staff Sgt. Dillard Johnson; John Matthews, Surefire; Mike Noell, BlackHawk Products Group;

Tom O'Connell, BlackHawk Products Group; First Sgt. Rudy Romero; Scott Sherwood, SOG Knives; Mike Sparks, www.combatreform.com; Col. Ricardo Riera, Garrison Commander, Fort Benning, Georgia; Sgt. Aaron Welch; and Jeff Wemmer, Spec-Ops Brand, and many more.

—Hans Halberstaft

CHAPTER ONE

A SOLDIER'S LOAD

For as long as common foot soldiers have marched off to battle, they have carried the same basic load—around eighty to a hundred pounds of weapons, armor, rations, digging tools, uniforms, and whatever else their sergeant thinks they ought to have handy when push comes to shove, and all of it digging into their shoulders through overloaded pack straps. Roman legionnaires carried eighty pounds of gear, and modern Rangers carry about the same or more. Both probably used similar profanity (although in different languages) to complain about it.

Left: Paratroopers and others have been using the ALICE rucksack for forty years, and even for training jumps, it is too damn heavy for comfort. These soldiers have been JMPI'd—jumpmaster personnel inspection—and struggle out to their aircraft with rucks weighing fifty pounds or so. In combat, they'd rig in flight, and the rucks would weigh twice as much.

ROTC cadets at Advance Camp are quickly introduced to ALICE and foot marches. These future officers get a small taste of life in the field. In the past, many of them would never have served in combat conditions; today, almost every one can expect a trip to the "sandbox" early in their career.

Nearly a hundred years after the M1910 system was adopted by the U.S. Army to connect canteens and bayonets to pistol belts, soldiers and Marines are still being issued gear nearly identical to the equipment worn during World War I.

entrenching tool and carrier, ammo cases scaled to the M14's twenty-round magazines, canteen cover and aluminum canteen, first-aid kit, and a sleeping-bag carrier. The pistol belt had a series of small grommets along the edges designed to accommodate the wire connectors on all the pouches and carriers, devices that went back to before World War I in U.S. Army service.

The big news for gear fans (if there were any) in 1967 was a redesign of the LCE, replacing the cotton and canvas with nylon and the brass buckle on the belt with a new stamped steel design dubbed the Davis buckle. The 1967 MLCE (*M* for modified) also featured new ammo pouches for the twenty- and thirty-round magazines used with the M16 rifle, and these were secured with a novel plastic latch that was easier to manipulate under stress. The plastic pistol belt buckle didn't come about until the mid-1980s and actually saw service on the ALICE frame first.

M1956 and M1967 LCE

Shortly after the end of the Korean War, the U.S. Army began to issue a set of components that were collectively known as the M1956 light-weight load-carrying equipment (LCE). The gear was based on the canvas-webbing pistol belt issued during World War II and added load-bearing suspenders, a small pack attached to the belt (called a butt pack then and now), an

ALICE and the Advent of Dummy Cord

The U.S. Army introduced a major new set of soldier gear in 1974, just a little too late to see much service in Vietnam. The pistol belt and all the rest of the M1967 gear were essentially unchanged, but the old M1910 wire-clip system for attaching components was replaced by an entirely new latch called the all-purpose lightweight individual

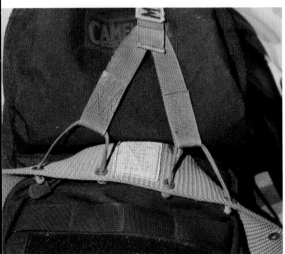

carrying equipment (ALICE) clip. These clips had a more rigid connection—when they stayed attached. Unfortunately, they came unclipped all by themselves, normally on patrol in the middle of the night, and knives, canteens, magazine pouches, and other bits of kit would fall to the ground, often unnoticed, only to be discovered in daylight. This problem encouraged soldiers and Marines to start tying everything to the load-bearing equipment (LBE) with parachute suspension cord, a very strong material about one-eighth of an inch in diameter. The parachute cord is commonly called 550 cord or dummy cord for its ability to keep you from looking like a dummy when you lose your pistol or Rambo knife. The remaining metal snaps were covered with the military version of duct tape, commonly called hundred-mile-an-hour tape for its ability to stay stuck.

New uniforms, vests, and helmets—Staff Sgt. Tyler Arnold, fashionably attired in the army's digital camouflage uniform and sporting LBV and MICH covers in matching ACU pattern.

Top left: Navy SEALs still use quite a lot of gear based on the M1910 system, including this Mk 3 Mod 0 dive knife shown here attached to a pistol belt. Such connections are normally either taped or tied down with "dummy cord" to prevent loss.

Lower left: Staff Sgt. Morrow prefers to use the M1967 gear but has wisely replaced the normal snaps and buckles with "stripped" 550 cord.

The joys of Ranger School's Mountain Phase still include the ALICE-Large ruck with enough gear and sandbags to make it cut into anybody's shoulders. It's 0500 and these students are off to learn all about rappelling.

The big development for the overall ALICE system was the introduction of two new backpacks, the medium and large rucksacks. Based on an external frame made of aluminum and a bag made of nylon, these rucks were rated at fifty- and seventy-pound capacities. Both are commonly used today, especially the large version, which—despite the rated capacity—often is loaded with 125 to 150 pounds of battlefield essentials: ammunition, batteries, and water.

Although the M1967 and ALICE gear seems highly out of date next to the new vests and rucks, all of it is still standard issue and very much in service in 2006.

Gucci Gear and Battle Rattle: A Fashion Revolution

There has been a radical change in the technology of the battlefield in recent years, and it is a kind of unofficial military secret. If you asked most

Americans where the latest technology was in the armed forces, they would probably tell you that it would be found in our helicopters, armored vehicles, missiles, and fighter aircraft. But they would be wrong. The CH-47 Chinook helicopter was designed fifty years ago, and so was the M16 rifle; the Abrams tank was designed thirty years ago. Many aircraft in combat today were built decades ago and have only been upgraded since.

The most radical changes on the battlefield can be found on the men and women themselves—the soldiers, Marines, air force rescue crews, SEALs, and explosive ordnance disposal (EOD) personnel. From head to foot, from the skin out, these men and women are using clothing and equipment that is entirely unlike anything other warriors have worn to war.

Not only that, these items of clothing and equipment have been developed and produced in an entirely new way, largely by private industry on its own initiative, quickly and without cost to the government. Twenty years or more ago, soldier gear was developed and tested by government agencies over many months and years, then it was constructed by one contractor and issued through the government supply system. That system is largely gone. Now, dozens of private companies compete with each other to design and manufacture boots, optics, weapon accessories, body armor, radios, flashlights, and many other items and then sell them directly to the end users, a system that is economical at many levels.

But perhaps the most remarkable part of this transformation is that individual warriors are spending their own money to purchase exotic and expensive equipment instead of accepting excellent gear issued by their parent unit. Many young soldiers and Marines spend hundreds or thousands of their own dollars on boots, vests, protective eyewear, assault packs, and knives, with various motivations. They don't need to do this—the U.S. Marine Corps, Army, Air Force, and Navy all provide extremely good clothing and tactical equipment—but there has evolved a sort of battlefield fashion that has generated a sense of warrior chic.

Soldiers and other military personnel call the gear they wear "battle rattle" because of all the little noises made by magazines rubbing together,

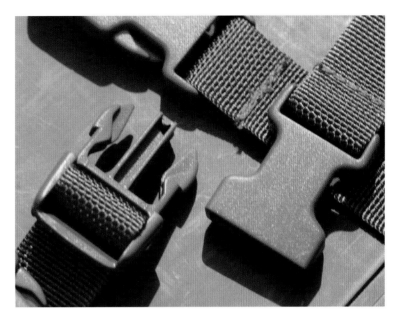

Fastex buckles in several sizes have largely displaced the old ALICE clip and M1910 wire hangers that previously attached one piece of gear to another.

The MOLLE or PALS system of straps, which weave together to connect pouches to packs and vests, has gradually gained acceptance by most—but not all—warfighters. It has allowed individual warriors to customize the position of individual pieces of gear on their load-bearing system in a way that was previously impossible.

This Marine is attired in the LandWarrior system, one of Natick Soldier Systems Center's goofier ideas. LandWarrior combines a small helmet-mounted display with short-range radios and a small computer intended to improve a dismounted squad's communications. His M16 rifle mounts a television camera, permitting him to fire from cover. The whole package, however, is excessively heavy, bulky, and delicate.

the squeaking of fabric as it is tensioned, the many noises a rifle makes as a magazine is seated in its well and as the charging handle is retracted and released to chamber a round. For the more expensive and elaborate items of equipment, especially those purchased with private funds, there is another term—"Gucci gear"—which applies to the $50 sunglasses with ballistic-protection lenses, the $200 three-day assault packs, the $150 boots, and the $550 knives. There is a kind of status today for the warrior with the most expensive gear, and some people, including some who don't really have a tactical mission, invest heavily in such fashionable attire. These people are sometimes called gear queers or geardos by their buddies who make do with equivalents issued by their unit.

Upper left: A legendary group of exceptionally brave warriors are the men of the explosive ordnance disposal (EOD) teams. This one has just boarded a ship the hard way, up a caving ladder; he wears a plate-carrier IBA, specialized EOD vest from London Bridge, a flotation device, retention lanyard for his M4 carbine (slung behind his back), pistol, knife, combination tool, and protective mask in a special watertight bag on his left leg. He's brought aboard a heavy ruck with the rest of the tools of his trade.

Above: Some soldiers still prefer the older ALICE-Large rucksack, including this sergeant at the U.S. Army Sniper School. He's got his CamelBak secured across the top flap instead of inside, one alternative method for hydration on the move.

One Soldier's Heavy Load: Operation Just Cause

At 0124 hours on the morning of December 20, 1989, the 3rd Battalion, 75th Ranger Regiment, conducted a parachute assault on Rio Hato Airport in the opening moments of Operation Just Cause in Panama. Maj. Charles Greene was a young sergeant back then and one of the battalion's snipers.

I was a squad leader at that time, and a sniper, too—roles we don't combine today. Most of the squad was assigned to be air-landed and drive our gun jeeps off the aircraft while my spotter and I were ordered to be part of the parachute assault. Even though there were just two of us from the squad, we were required to have enough ammunition for the complete squad to complete its mission, even if just the two of us had to do it ourselves. The result of that order was that we both had to repack our rucks, discarding a lot of gear we normally carried and replacing it with ammunition. Capt. Tony Thomas, my company commander, had jumped into Grenada and had learned the lesson of overloaded rucks then. He tried to get control of the weight issue for this jump, but it was too late, and the senior NCOs, who had not made combat jumps before, overloaded us. Thomas came around with his scale, and my ALICE-Large ruck weighed exactly 126 pounds. When he discovered this could not be corrected and that we would jump with those weights, he stormed off in anger.

That load included two LAWs (light antitank weapons), two 60mm mortar rounds, 600 rounds of M60 machine-gun ammunition, four SAW ammunition drums containing 800 rounds, six M67 fragmentation grenades, two thermite grenades—and those things are heavy!—a basic load of ammunition for my M16, 210 rounds of 5.56mm in seven mags. There were 110 rounds of M118 ball 7.62mm ammunition for my sniper rifle, even though the rifle itself would be delivered on one of our gun jeeps.

I also carried quite a lot of explosives— two blocks of C-4, blasting caps, det [detonation] cord, time fuse and fuse lighters, and two M18 Claymore mines. The explosives were prepared for use with a blasting cap crimped to a thirty-second length of time fuse and a fuse-igniter attached to the other end; I carried two of these in one pocket on the right side of my uniform and two charges in the pocket on the left side.

Then there was an E-tool (entrenching tool, a compact, folding shovel), the heaviest thing in anybody's ruck, two two-quart canteens of water, and a poncho. My normal personal gear all had to be removed to make room for the ammunition and explosives. This was in late December, and it was cold, about twenty degrees, but all our snivel gear was thrown in a pile to be hauled away.

One of the things I lost was my poncho liner, and I paid dearly for that! Every Ranger loves his poncho liner, but I had to get rid of it to make room for the ammo. It was really hot during the day, but at night, when the temperature dropped twenty or thirty degrees, you feel like you are freezing to death. I got to keep the poncho only and ended up having to share one poncho as a blanket for both me and my spotter on the brief times we were allowed to sleep. I am never without my 'cho liner now, and when I fly someplace, one is in my carry-on bag just in case I get stuck someplace or the plane goes down. It is the perfect thing to keep you comfortable when it gets cold.

Each of us wore our standard LBE over BDUs. On mine I carried two M16 magazine pouches, four fragmentation grenades, a flashlight, and a butt pack containing a cleaning kit for my rifle and enough food items from an MRE to make one meal. A bayonet for the M16 was also on the LBE, and it was amazingly sharp after three days of honing.

This basic load for the M16 annoyed me, because, as a sniper, I thought I should have had a lot more 7.62mm ammunition for my primary weapon. My rifle was a standard M16A2, but had a Litton night sight, zeroed just prior to departure for the airfield. The M24 sniper rifle had not then been certified to be jumped, so it was on a gun jeep waiting to be air-landed; I got it about four hours after we landed. Until it arrived, I had to make do with the M16.

Because of the long flight, we combat-rigged in flight. I was one of the jumpmasters and the second man out. When it came time to hook that rucksack on me, I couldn't stand up at first and only got up with a lot of effort. When it came time to move to the door, I could just waddle forward a few steps, and then drop the ruck to the floor. I finally got to the door and instead of getting a good door position, I just fell out. The canopy opened and took up the entire load, and that was a godsend. I pulled the releases to lower the ruck almost immediately. Drop altitude was just 450 feet, so we were not in the air very long, just a few seconds. We all left our rucks on the drop zone, and they stayed there until the next day when people went around with jeeps to pick them up.

This ruck, worn by a member of 2nd Battalion, 8th Infantry Regiment, 4th Infantry Division, illustrates the problem of the soldier's load—everything but the kitchen sink, and maybe that, too, is included—sleeping-bag system, pad, NVG, MREs, water, gas mask, batteries, medic bag, and more. A soldier can move a load like this, but not quickly and not far and not with the strength needed to engage in combat on arrival. When it was tried during Operation Anaconda in Afghanistan, the result was a tactical disaster and a major lesson relearned.

Balancing the Load

Ground-combat operations require a terrible compromise between resources that a warrior needs on the battlefield and the cost of getting them there, the art of logistics. You would think that today, in the age of helicopter transport, lightweight composite materials, and space-age alloys, the individual soldier's load would be substantially reduced. That's what a lot of people predicted when the M16 rifle, weighing about nine pounds including a full thirty-round magazine, replaced the M14 rifle, which weighed eleven pounds with a full twenty-round magazine. The new lightweight rifle and ammunition

This captain and his soldiers have dropped their rucks several hundred meters short of their objective and are now moving up to breach an obstacle with explosive "Bangalore torpedoes" while the fortifications burn in the background, the result of artillery prep just concluded.

were supposed to lighten the soldier's burden substantially, but it didn't turn out that way. Instead, soldiers were weighed down with more ammunition, and their load remained essentially the same.

The soldier's individual load is part of a fundamental struggle on the battlefield, the conflict between agility and sustainability. On one extreme, we see today's insurgents with an RPG or AK-47 and a magazine or two, dressed in T-shirt and pants, wearing sandals, conducting military operations in Iraq and Afghanistan. They don't have armor, helmets, assault packs, first-aid kits, hydration systems, or all the other high-tech/cool-guy stuff considered standard equipment by their opponents. These insurgents are tremendously agile, get their food and water and

ammunition resupplied from the local population, and have almost no logistical train at all.

The American and British warfighters, on the other hand, carry a minimum of seven magazines or 210 rounds for their M4 carbines, they wear torso armor and helmets, a radio, grenades, one or more knives, and a lot of additional kit that typically weighs forty to sixty pounds.

The soldier's load has always had two parts. One is the fighting load, the tools of the trade when actually engaged in combat; the other is the approach load, all the items needed to keep a warrior out in the field for an extended period.

Fighting Load

A modern American, British, or Israeli soldier with a ground-combat mission carries forty to sixty

A combat engineer, carrying a reasonable fighting load, moves toward his objective.

pounds of ammunition, a primary weapon, a secondary weapon, water, torso armor, a helmet, a radio, and a first-aid kit. The fighting load will often include a few fragmentation grenades, a few smoke grenades, and a small amount of food, perhaps enough for one meal or snack. With this load, the soldier is expected to be able to operate as part of a fire team, squad, or platoon for up to one day of patrolling or an hour or so of combat. According to the U.S. Army, the total of all the items carried by the individual warrior—including boots, underwear, and uniform—should be kept under forty-eight pounds, and generally it is.

Approach Load

The approach load has been driving soldiers and their leaders crazy for years. It is all the stuff that goes in the big rucksack, and it typically includes a lot of rifle ammunition, a couple of 60mm mortar rounds, M18 Claymore mines, spare boots, spare clothing, medical items, MREs (meal, ready to eat), water, batteries, spare smoke and fragmentation grenades, snivel gear (anything that keeps you from freezing to death or even merely comfortable under cold and wet conditions, such

Above: Side view of the ALICE-Large ruck. When loaded with ammo, batteries, and water, they can weigh eighty or one hundred pounds. The external aluminum frame allows good ventilation but is sometimes bent or broken.

M18 smoke grenades are available in several types and colors, each of which weighs about one pound. Squad and platoon leaders often carry one or more on their LBV and more in their assault pack or ruck.

as sleeping bags and ponchos), and other items for both tactical and personal use.

Ordinarily, the approach load will be carried in a large rucksack, either the ALICE large or the newer military versions of the backpack. These rucks turn soldiers into a sort of mule; they carry this load to some point near where the enemy is expected to be attacked, then drop the rucksack and make the attack wearing just the fighting load.

The U.S. Army currently says that the soldier's total load should not normally exceed seventy-two pounds—fighting load and rucksack load combined—for an approach march when the soldier is expected to fight on arrival. Only in emergencies should an approach load be allowed to get up to 120 to 150 pounds. But these weights have been vastly exceeded during current combat operations, especially in Operation Anaconda.

RECON Marines are respected by members of all the U.S. armed forces for their legendary courage, discipline, and combat reconnaissance skills. They also carry among the heaviest rucks in the warfighting business.

Operation Anaconda: Lessons Learned

As a good example of the way soldiers' load lessons have to be relearned at the beginning of every war, First Sgt. Rudy Romero of Bravo Company, 1/187th Infantry, 101st Airborne Division, wrote a report on his unit's experiences during Operation Anaconda in Afghanistan in 2002. The 101st had trained long and hard for combat, including many long visits to the Joint Readiness Training Center (JRTC) at Fort Polk, Louisiana, and they thought they were up to speed.

Bravo Company had trained to fight combat light at JRTC, but when assigned to Operation Anaconda, they found themselves burdened with huge rucks that were so heavy that virtually all the men in the company were exhausted within hours of insertion. Part of the problem was the altitude, part was the terrain, and part was the cold wind. Soldiers know how to deal with all these factors and have access to suitable boots and other gear, but in the confusion of a first real combat operation, old lessons get forgotten and new gear sometimes gets left behind.

Some members of the battalion left sleeping bags out of their rucks and planned to make do with cold-weather underwear (polypro), Gore-Tex jackets and pants, and gloves. In the high altitude and with high winds, these things were not enough and the unit had hypothermia cases bad enough to require evacuation.

Staff Sgt. Campbell provides a firsthand account of what he calls an Operation Anaconda "hike from hell."

We were so overloaded on Operation Anaconda that every one of us ended up using our weapons as a staff for support. I thought I had been through some tough stuff during the pre-Ranger program, but that was nothing compared to what we went through in Afghanistan. I had about six belts of SAW [squad automatic weapon] ammo in my ruck, six magazines of 5.56mm ammo besides the seven on my vest, two 60mm mortar rounds, and enough batteries and water to make the ruck weight alone about 120 pounds. Even though we knew conditions would be very cold, there wasn't enough room in the ruck for a sleeping bag—all I had was polypro underwear, Gore-Tex, and a poncho liner.

We walked day and night for two days with those immense loads, but we were barely moving. We brought too much ammunition and not nearly enough food; my squad shared two MREs between eleven guys one night; I got the package of Skittles for dinner, other guys were eating the coffee and anything with nutritional value.

I was one of the few who put the pouches directly on my IBA [interceptor body armor]. It seemed like a good idea at the time, but when we were digging in, the other guys could shed their vests and keep the armor for protection, but I had to dig while wearing all that ammo, frags, and smoke grenades. It got in the way and made the whole process harder.

Common sense should have prevented the load problems. It was obvious just walking to the helicopters that the loads were out of control. I was waiting for our platoon sergeants to stand up and say something, but none of them did. When people were falling out just trying to get out to the helicopters, somebody should have stood up and insisted on leaving some of the load behind, but nobody did. During the AAR (after-action review) later on, the load problem was brought up, but the real lesson learned was that nobody had the courage to say something when there was a chance to fix the issue. (The platoon sergeants were the ones responsible, in my opinion, not the senior commanders, who have other things to think about.)

Optimum Loads and Packing Lists

For many years, and after many studies and tests, the optimum load for any soldier has been established at 30 percent of his body weight. Commanders know this, and so do the sergeants who make the packing lists the soldiers use when they prepare their gear for a mission. But the knowledge competes with a distrust of the supply system's ability to resupply ammunition, water, and batteries, so the sergeants tend to order heavier loads than actually needed and tell the soldiers to suck it up.

When Lt. Col. Charles Dean went to Afghanistan in 2004 to see what 82nd Airborne Division soldiers were actually carrying, he found that riflemen were carrying sixty-three pounds

Above: Officers attending the 18-Alpha component of the Q-course rehearse an operation that will launch the following night. They will parachute into remote terrain with these rucks, each weighing around eighty pounds.

Top: A rifleman's basic load is 210 rounds of 5.56mm ammo—seven magazines if you cram each full to its thirty-round capacity, or eight if you're smart and avoid compressing the spring completely and risking a stoppage. Each mag weighs about one pound and, depending on the mission, an operator may carry twelve or more mags, each adding to their load.

Above: One can of .50-caliber HEI (high-explosive-incendiary) used by M107 snipers holds only sixty rounds but adds many pounds to the rucks of the team, which are already heavily burdened.

Left: Soldiers from 2/8 4ID conduct a live-fire exercise while wearing heavy and ineffective flak-jacket body armor on a 100-plus-degree afternoon. Flak jackets, originating in World War II, have been displaced by interceptor body armor, which combines Kevlar vests with ceramic armor plates for more stopping power with less weight.

Staff Sgt. Tim Johns runs down the road with his ruck and twenty-eight-pound M107 Barrett .50-caliber rifle.

for their fighting load, well over his 30-percent optimum. The riflemen's approach load was ninety-six pounds—55 percent of their body weight. Emergency approach march loads in Dean's study averaged 127 pounds for riflemen, but were even worse for members of 60mm mortar teams, who carried loads of 147 pounds, almost their average body weight. All these figures exceed what everybody knows warriors should be carrying, and all the players understand how and why the loads grow. But the rucksacks continue to get even bigger, and the packing lists get longer and heavier in units that have not experienced much combat. The loads diminish somewhat after the opening moves of most combat operations, once the logistics system gets itself unscrewed, and the sergeants

acquire experience about what really needs to be on the soldier's back and what can be brought in on a supply helicopter.

Solving the Load-Planning Problem

There are many ways to look at the load issue, and soldiers have tried them all in an effort to get control of the burden. Even when trimming packing lists to what seems to be only essentials, the totals can be appalling. Below is how one noncommissioned officer (NCO) from an air-defense unit broke down the issue for members of his unit:

This is a very disciplined load and leaves out a great deal of gear that is considered essential for field operations. But it also adds some items that are not typical for most warfighters—SINCGARS,

Common items (battle dress uniform [BDU], underwear, boots, one MRE)	**15.00 pounds**
Environmental protection (poncho, liner, two-quart canteen of water)	**11.70 pounds**
Duty load (M16A2, seven magazines, two grenades)	**18.30 pounds**
Threat protection (helmet, mask)	**9.66 pounds**
Mission load (ALICE-Large, a single-channel ground and airborne radio system [SINCGARS], GPS, binoculars, Stinger missile)	**64.55 pounds**
TOTAL for Stinger team leader	**119.21 pounds**

For long-range, secure, reliable voice and data communication on the battlefield, warfighters use the SINCGARS (Single Channel Ground and Airborne Radio System). The basic weight of the radio is 26 pounds, a substantial load for the soldiers who carry them along with their basic load of ammunition and water.

Much of a soldier's load is made up of things that might be life-savers or mission-essential equipment that are carried along just in case. This includes explosives for destroying bunkers and enemy munitions.

binoculars, and especially the Stinger missile. But members of other units find their loads increased, often to much higher totals, with things like mortar base plates, mortar rounds, far more rifle ammunition, twice the water, plus smoke and fragmentation grenades, light antitank weapons (LAWs), and Claymores. Most soldiers today would discard the protective mask as useless but would add interceptor body armor (IBA).

Warfighters report that the issue of overloading is alive and well, but is much better managed now than it was at the outset of ground-combat operations in Iraq. The U.S. Army and Marine Corps have been applying those lessons learned.

Tactical leaders—officers and NCOs—have learned to show greater discipline about mission planning. Instead of trying to carry enough for every possible contingency, they plan to carry what is needed for the actual mission to be performed under the actual conditions forecast for the operation. The essential ammo, water, and gear are carried, and the rest is left out of the rucks and assault packs.

Units have learned to trust the logistics system and to depend on it to bring ammunition, water, batteries, and even snivel gear on helicopters or trucks, in a timely manner.

Even foot patrols now have one or two vehicles nearby for support. One is a "war wagon" with extra ammunition for rifles and machine guns, fragmentation and smoke grenades, Claymores, pop flares, and a .50-caliber squad automatic weapon (SAW), M240, or Mk 19 in a turret mount to provide heavier firepower if the patrol gets into trouble. All that ammo and additional firepower relieves the guys on foot from carrying anything more than what they really need for the mission of the moment. Some foot patrols have a second humvee, typically called a chow wagon, with cases of bottled water, boxes of MREs, combat lifesaver bags, and other support items that don't have to be carried by the individual rifleman.

Center and left: Belted ammunition for the squad's automatic weapons, and lots of spare ammo for M4 carbines and M16 rifles, are also prominent among the various deadly items that warfighters might carry. Each of these items, including grenades and mines, weighs only a pound or so, but the pounds add up for every American warfighter.

The need for long-range, unsupported, foot-patrol operations similar to Operation Anaconda in 2002 has largely disappeared. Insertions are done by helicopter far more frequently now; warfighters still may have 130-pound rucks and 170-pound total loads, but they don't often need to move them long distances as was common a few years ago.

Some gear is now shared instead of duplicated. When sleeping bags are required, units now only carry enough for soldiers who will be asleep at any one time. Since that might be only half the unit while the other half is pulling security, the total load is diminished substantially.

Food and water discipline during operations is different from peacetime operations. Three MREs are normal daily issue in garrison; one or two are normal for short periods on combat operations. Water purification tablets and filter pumps are much lighter than even one quart of water and can treat many gallons of stream water or melted snow. Heavier loads are rotated at intervals to keep from exhausting warfighters.

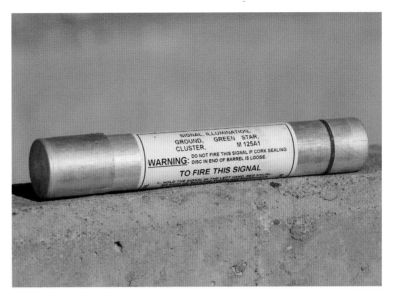

There will almost always be some pop flares stowed in a patrolling platoon's assault packs or rucksacks. Pop flares are used to signal attacks and withdrawals, normally at night but in the day as well. The rocket flies up to about 300 feet where it ejects a cluster of pyrotechnic stars or a flare attached to a small parachute. The effect is not subtle and everybody in range will know you are up to something.

For the EOD teams, part of their battle rattle is a laptop computer, one tool required to deal with the many kinds of threats encountered by these teams.

CHAPTER TWO

FIRST LINE GEAR

Marines call it first-line gear—the individual's tactical clothing, boots, footgear, and headgear. As with everything else, a lot of people have put a lot of thought into what works best for the most warfighters, and, as usual, there are a variety of opinions on the subject.

We need to start by mentioning unmentionables, or underwear. Since tactical operations are conducted now in very adverse conditions, a lot of research and development money has been invested in these garments. All the services are issuing undergarments

Left: Today's warfighter demands battlefield fashion that fits his or her action-packed lifestyle, like the classic battle dress uniform shown here in the ever-popular woodland camouflage pattern. Worn by members of all the U.S. armed forces until recently, BDUs are finally being left in the back of the closet by many warriors anxious for something new and fresh, and they've found it in competing "digital cammies" from the USMC and the House of Natick.

undergarments designed to provide as much comfort as possible while also protecting the wearer against battlefield threats like fire.

Many warfighters have been buying Under Armor and similar garments that are very effective at wicking away perspiration and keeping the wearer relatively cool in hot climates. "When the army went to the RFI, we were issued black Under Armor briefs," one soldier said. "I decided to give them a try. Before that, like most guys, I didn't wear briefs at all because of the ventilation issue. Now I am a convert; [it is] the most comfortable underwear available."

These shirts and shorts are quite expensive, four or five times the cost of conventional cotton equivalents, but are popular items in the exchanges and in the military catalog and Web sales. The Marine Corps, however, banned their use in 2006 because the material can melt when

exposed to the flash of an improvised explosive device (IED); the result is skin damage even worse than that caused by the explosion directly. However, Marines argue that by reducing casualties from flash burns, more casualties from heat stress will be caused. Soldiers, at this writing, may still wear Under Armor and similar fabrics.

Well, this is a little military secret: Navy SEALs and many others in SOF and other units don't wear underwear. "I don't wear undershorts and haven't since I became a Ranger," Maj. Charles Greene reports. With SEALs, the tradition goes back to basic underwater demolition/SEAL student (BUD/S) training when each student spends a lot of time in the surf and the dunes getting wet and sandy. The sand gets inside clothing, where it acts like sandpaper, and the logical thing to do is to make it as easy as possible for the sand to migrate down the pant leg or under

the BDU shirt. Underwear collects the sand, so most SEALs don't wear it.

Some very expensive underwear is now available for those who do want to wear it. The army is currently preparing to issue a new set of garments designed by the Natick Soldier Systems Center and based on reports from Afghanistan. The garments are similar to those available commercially and used by mountaineers and others engaged in outdoor sports. Natick calls the system the protective combat uniform (PCU); it has seven levels and is expected to replace the existing SPEAR (special-operations forces equipment advanced requirements) garments in current issue. SEALs, RECON Marines, Rangers, and

The floppy hat was introduced about forty years ago and remains an essential part of the modern warfighter's wardrobe. Some SEALs get theirs from overseas.

Also known as a boonie hat, it can be shaped in many ways, all the while keeping rain and bugs from falling down your neck and providing a bit of shade for the eyes.

The floppy hat can even be accessorized to make a fashion statement.

Green Berets evaluated the PCU clothing before its approval.

This new issued protective clothing is one small part of a massive lesson-learned response to warfighters' experiences in Afghanistan and Iraq. Operation Anaconda taught some brutal lessons in proper attire for sustained combat operations at high altitude, and many of the soldiers and Marines who participated in the mission had severe problems with the 10,000-foot and higher altitudes, high winds, and subfreezing temperatures.

While the special-operations guys and gals will be getting the high-tech clothing through the supply system, the rest are often buying their own through commercial outlets. The most popular of several brands of such clothing is Under Armor, a company that produces expensive gear for athletes and has adapted its microfiber T-shirts, shorts, and socks, as well as underwear, for military wear in both cold- and hot-weather environments. The PCU gear provided by the supply system costs the warrior nothing, while the commercial T-shirts cost $25 each and other garments currently run up to $55. Despite the cost, lots of military personnel spend the money to gain a little comfort.

Digital Cammies: MARPAT and ACU

The entire American military community has been wearing woodland-pattern clothing since 1981, and the military forces of many other nations have adopted quite similar uniforms. There have been variations over the years—the six-color desert pattern used during the first Gulf War was replaced by a three-color desert pattern in the 1990s. Then, in 2004, the Marine Corps introduced a radically new version of the tactical uniform, the MARPAT (Marine disruptive pattern) uniform. Quickly dubbed "digital cammies" because of the uniform's characteristic pattern, the Corps suddenly had a very striking and distinctive tactical uniform that took the battlefield fashion world by storm. The pattern was so unusual that the Marine Corps protected it by copyright, preventing the production of imitations or knockoffs.

There were originally three variants of the MARPAT digital cammies: one to replace the old woodland pattern of dark green, brown, and black; a desert pattern comprising shades of tan and brown; and an urban pattern featuring shades of gray. The last version, however, was discontinued because the Marine Corps felt it was redundant.

There are many kinds of uniforms in use, some of which look pretty strange out of context. This U.S. Army Sniper School student is using a "ghillie" suit which he made using old BDUs and other materials.

These new patterns got a lot of positive attention. They would have been fine for all the Armed Forces, just as the old BDUs had been, but instead all the branches have developed digital cammies of their own. All look a lot like the MARPAT, with very slight variations in color. The air force has its version with a lot of blue, the navy's has blues and grays, and the army's is all shades of gray. This latter is the new army combat uniform (ACU) and is, at this writing, displacing the old BDUs at a fairly rapid rate.

ACUs are cut quite differently than BDUs, and soldiers generally have nice things to say about the fit and comfort of the new uniform.

They like the placement of the pockets, especially the one on the left sleeve cuff designed for pens and pencils, as well as the shoulder-mounted pockets that can be accessed while wearing body armor and combat equipment. Navy SEALs have been modifying their BDUs with these shoulder pockets for years, and now the pockets have finally been incorporated into their issue uniforms.

Gloves

Gloves are important warrior wear. Operators and a great many people with all sorts of tactical missions wear gloves in hot weather or cold. Ground personnel originally wore the same thin leather gloves worn by aviators decades ago. These gloves were intended to provide some protection in case of fire.

Traditional uniforms and web gear are now being gradually displaced by tactical vests and the ACU pattern. Staff Sgt. Aaron Welch gives the secret 10th Mountain Division recognition signal while wearing the very chic ACU accessorized with contrasting tactical vest from Central Issue Facility in desert tan.

In 1963, a material called Nomex was introduced and was soon used in the production of protective garments for flight crews. Nomex flight gloves are now found on many thousands of Marines, soldiers, and others who have no aircrew assignments, because the gloves keep hands protected against abrasion and wick away perspiration. Riflemen often cut off the tips of the glove fingers to provide better trigger control when firing.

Years ago, these gloves were routinely liberated from aviation units, then became available through retail outlets like U.S. Cavalry and Ranger Joe's, two companies that pioneered service to the tactical-military marketplace. Several manufacturers noticed the market for these gloves and started making similar ones. Both Hatch and BlackHawk offer a huge line of specialized gloves, some with Kevlar to protect against sharp objects, others with heavy insulation, and others designed for wet environments. The old flight glove is now available in many variants, some with long gauntlets to protect the wrist and forearm, and others that end right at the wrist. The index finger on many versions has stitching that permits the tip to be cut back without the material unraveling. U.S. Cavalry currently

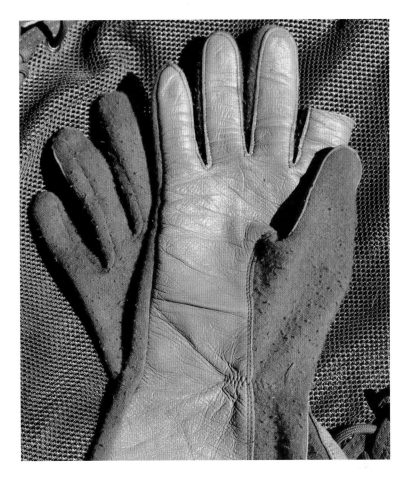

Above: Snipers wear gloves to protect their hands during a long stalk and provide a bit of camouflage. Originally designed for aircraft crews, these goatskin and Nomex gloves immediately found favor with Green Berets, SEALs, and many others in the conflict-resolution business. Warfighters frequently cut off the tip of the glove's index finger for extra dexterity and trigger control.

Left: Jim, a Navy SEAL, demonstrates that fingerless gloves originally designed for rock climbing serve equally well when operating an M4 during a drill.

offers about a hundred different glove designs, each in multiple sizes.

Despite all the product-development efforts of the tactical-clothing vendors, a lot of SEALs and other warfighters get their gloves at the hardware and auto-repair store. The gloves they are buying are designed for auto mechanics and offer excellent dexterity and durability. And they cost about $15 a pair instead of $30 and up, like those from tactical-clothing vendors.

Helmets and Kevlars

About 20 percent of injuries to warfighters today are to the head, and include ballistic, fragmentation, and other kinds of impact injuries. Despite the weight and other handicaps of helmets, most military personnel are glad to wear them. The PASGT (personal armor system, ground troops) helmet is current standard issue in the army and Marine Corps, but will gradually be replaced by about 2007.

The PASGT helmet was introduced in the early 1980s and created a small tempest at the time because of its resemblance to the German helmet of World War II. It was called, for a time, the "Fritz" helmet because of this similarity. The shape did a good job of protecting a soldier's head, but many felt that American soldiers should not look like Nazis under any circumstances, even for safety.

The soldiers didn't worry about the visual similarity. They liked the helmet immediately for a couple of reasons. The first was that it was much more comfortable than the M1 helmet of World War II it replaced; the second was that it proved it could save lives by stopping bullets. Rangers and members of the 82nd Airborne were among the first to be issued the new Kevlar helmet

Upper left: Although the Kevlar is normally worn with a cover, but is sometimes as bare as the Roster Alpha 223 that 2nd Lt. Van Camp demonstrates at the Basic Airborne Course.

Left: The PAGST or Kevlar or "k-pot" has been issued for about twenty years. The Kevlar provides pretty good ballistic protection and is far more comfortable than the steel pot it replaced.

shortly before Operation Urgent Fury, the attack on Grenada in 1983. One of these helmets famously stopped a projectile from an AK during the assault; the impact knocked the soldier down, but he was otherwise uninjured. His helmet was on display at the 82nd Airborne Division museum at Fort Bragg, North Carolina, and the incident helped develop confidence in the PASGT, soon informally christened the "Kevlar."

In the eternal tradition of soldiers, they do have some complaints about the Kevlar. The suspension system is much more comfortable than that of the old "steel pot," but since nobody in today's army or Marine Corps today has worn one of those, the comparison is academic, and they want something better. A foam doughnut cushion is widely used and helps. But the big complaint is a tactical one—the back of the helmet is frequently pushed forward by a rucksack or body armor when the soldier or Marine is firing from the prone position, interfering badly with proper use of a weapon.

In the late 1990s, these issues resulted in a development process to modify the Kevlar, and a new helmet, the modular/integrated communications helmet (MICH), began to be issued in 2001. It is currently replacing the Kevlar across the army, and soldiers generally love it. The Marine Corps is working on its own version.

The MICH is considerably lighter than the Kevlar. A set of six to eight foam pads backed with Velcro provide support and can be mixed and matched to suit the individual's head. Some of these pads can be removed as needed when the user wants to accommodate a low-profile communications headset. The back of the MICH

Upper right: Tankers wear a different kind of protective headgear, the CVC or combat vehicle crewman helmet. The CVC has commo systems built in. It is being worn here by 4ID M2 Bradley crews decontaminating their vehicles after a simulated chemical attack.

Right: The MICH helmet is lighter and more comfortable than the Kevlar, with pads inside instead of a webbing suspension.

is cut a bit higher than the Kevlar and doesn't conflict with rucks or body armor, though it doesn't protect the back of the head quite as well, either.

Unlike the old Kevlar, MICH helmets are sometimes worn in combat and in garrison without a camouflage cover, a practice that varies with units. Special forces detachments went into combat in 2003 with bare MICH helmets.

Eye Protection

The threat from IEDs on the modern battlefield has changed another kind of gear warfighters are wearing—eye protection, or eyepro, as it is

The MICH was designed to be compatible with headsets; the Kevlar was not. The MICH uses a slightly different mount for night-vision goggles; the bracket for the NVG clips onto the mount on the front center of the helmet.

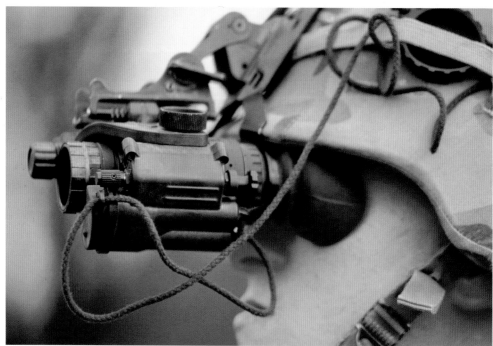

Once mounted on the helmet, the NVG can be lowered into position as needed.

This soldier's glasses are certified for use while conducting parachute operations and are compatible with a helmet but provide no protection from side impact. Eyewear in the army has previously been limited to a small selection of designs that were sturdy but not exactly something you'd wear on a date. Soldiers have long called the standard-issue frames *BCGs*—birth-control glasses.

Several vendors produce goggles specifically for military use and have therefore adjusted the shape of the goggles to fit the MICH helmet better. The material used for the lenses is amazingly tough, and all the major vendors have testimonials from warfighters reporting incidents of saved eyesight. The lenses in this set from ESS, which currently seems to be the most popular brand on the battlefield, will stop shotgun pellets fired from close range.

SEALs are pioneers in battlefield fashion, partly because of their budgets, partly because they have more latitude about what they wear to social functions. Here, Jim is dressed to kill with his Oakley glasses, a dominant brand in the battlefield market and certified to protect the eyes from both front and side impacts. Helmets are often dispensed with in favor of ball caps, especially in training but sometimes in battle. While having the bill backward may be only a fashion statement in the city, on the range it keeps hot brass from dropping down the back of your neck.

commonly called. This gear is part of first-line equipment. Not too many years ago, the use of sunglasses on patrol operations was considered inappropriate and was discouraged or prohibited. That has changed dramatically, partially because of battlefield conditions and partially because of lessons learned from law-enforcement and SOF units.

Goggles have been issued since World War II, and the same basic design has stayed in the supply system for nearly half a century. Those goggles used a rubber frame, elastic headband,

and thin plastic lenses. The frame invariably bunched up, the lenses fogged up, and the elastic was pitifully weak.

Sometime in the 1980s, navy SEALs started using goggles designed for downhill skiing. SEALs have goggles because they use nonlethal distraction devices called flash-bangs. Flash-bangs produce a fair amount of smoke and sometimes spray a lot of debris in the enclosed spaces where they are deployed. Both the smoke and debris are hazardous to the eyes. While the skiing goggles were not designed for tactical

Eye protection, or *eyepro* as the warfighters call it, is a big part of the cool-guy factor in the box. Here's a Dane with a bad attitude, an M4, and some cool Wiley X goggles. *Wiley X*

use and were not up to industrial standards for protective eyewear, they were far superior to the existing goggle design. Special operations personnel with close-quarters battle (CQB) missions, like SEALs conducting vessel boarding/search/seizure missions, were happy to have them.

Once again, the recreation-equipment industry noticed a new potential market and started redesigning products originally intended for fun to the deadly business of tactical operations. Bollé, ESS (Eye Safety System, Inc.), Wiley X, Revision, and Oakley all currently provide protective eyewear to American tactical units, and Natick has developed a version of its own.

Protective eyewear is extremely popular with military personnel on tactical missions, who are all aware of the risks from blast fragments, ultraviolet (UV) radiation, dust, wind, tree branches, two kinds of lasers, infrared (IR) light, and pro-

jectiles of many kinds. Sixteen percent of injuries in the "sandbox" of Iraq are eye related. The use of approved eyewear is now mandatory in most units, with no complaints from the troops. Soldiers and Marines often wear goggles with clear lenses during night operations. The "cool guy" factor with most commercial, off-the-shelf (COTS) eyepro is very high.

And the level of protection is also very high. Current eyepro from all leading manufacturers will stop shotgun pellets fired from about thirty feet, as well as passing other standardized tests. The military has circulated photographs of personnel who have been injured in the face by

Everybody may be wearing exactly the same helmet, uniform, body armor, and carrying the same weapon, but sunglasses like these Wiley Xs are in huge demand, both as protection against the elements and battlefield hazards, and because most guys think they look really great.

Wiley X

Wiley X is one of the pioneers in the military and law-enforcement eyepro market. Their glasses and goggles are among the most popular for both issue and personal purchase by today's warriors. Hundreds of thousands of these products are produced by the family-owned company, which got started in 1987 making shooting glasses for a few FBI agents in one office. Other law-enforcement agencies noticed those first ballistic-resistant glasses, and the Wiley X product line expanded and evolved. The company concentrated on ballistic protection from the start rather than adapting a recreational product to industrial standards, like other companies.

The 82nd Airborne Division was one of the first units to order Wiley X eyewear in bulk, buying thousands of the company's SG-1s shortly before deployment to Afghanistan in late spring of 2002. The SG-1 is a compact, low-profile goggle that can be converted to sunglasses by removing the headband and snapping on temple pieces. Though the first big order was from the paratroopers, Wiley X originally developed the SG-1 for the Ranger regiment.

"The Rangers had already been buying our glasses for years and liked them," says Dan Freeman, Wiley X's vice president of marketing. "But they approached us and said, 'We'd like to have you design something for us that we can wear while jumping from an aircraft, but still wear when we get on the ground.'"

The SG-1 was the result of that request and a two-year development process.

Wiley X is currently developing more eye-protection products. It has recently launched a new very-low-profile goggle called the Nerve, as well as a new ballistic shield, the PT-3, which incorporates a new prescription-lens carrier that fits both goggle and spectacle configurations.

The Barrett sniper rifle is designed to knock out thin-skinned vehicles and similar targets at up to a mile or so; when it fires, the muzzle break vents propellant gases to the side and rear, kicking up a lot of gravel and sand. Eye protection is standard when shooting such weapons, in this case a kind of combination of sunglasses and goggles made by ESS.

blasts of debris and shrapnel, but whose eyes have been saved by their eyepro; their skin is peppered with small impacts and wounds, but the outline of their protective eyewear is revealed by a mask of undamaged skin.

Ear Protection

Old combat soldiers, particularly artillerymen, are famous for bad hearing caused by prolonged exposure to high noise levels. In an effort to protect against such noise, warfighters use hearing protection that ranges from simple earplugs to custom-fitted inserts and headsets that permit the transmission of low sound levels while blocking the high levels characteristic of gunfire and explosions.

Hearing protection can be as simple as foam earplugs or as sophisticated as these Peltor muffs, which allow the user to hear normal conversations and whispers but electronically remove loud noises like weapons discharge.

Footwear
Socks

A lot of money is spent on socks by soldiers, and they are not buying the issue socks. Soldiers are spending good money on civilian alternatives because their feet are their greatest asset.

Some socks have Kevlar reinforcement, made from polyester, nylon, and a lot of other materials, again based on lessons learned from the outdoor-recreation industry. These high-tech—or *high-speed*, as modern warfighters like to say—socks cost up to $30 per pair, but the warriors seem to think they are a good investment, because the expensive socks are keeping their feet comfortable and healthy in the very difficult conditions found in Iraq and Afghanistan.

Boots

Gone are the days of the spit-shined jump boot. Every service has abandoned the smooth leather combat boot in favor of suede footwear of various designs. While the military had been issuing tan rough-out leather desert boots since the first Gulf War, the Marine Corps led the pack in developing a general-issue suede combat boot. Their first effort was a Mojave Green suede version of their Gore-Tex–lined infantry combat boot featuring an eagle, globe, and anchor branded into the heel—the Marine Corps combat boot (temperate). This was soon followed by a boot to replace both the desert and jungle boots—the Marine Corps combat boot (hot weather). When the army adopted the ACU, it also adopted a low-maintenance tan boot that is quite similar to the Marine Corps boot. As the navy adopts its new digital pattern utility uniform it will begin to issue a black rawhide work boot, and the air force, not to be outdone, has set their sights on a sage green jungle-style boot.

Upper left: Besides the abrasion of rocks in Afghanistan and sand in Iraq, the boots worn by warfighters have to hold up to prolonged immersion in water without failure. The jungle boot designed in the 1960s is still preferred for such conditions.

Left: While many soldiers accept the issued desert boots from Central Issue, the quality of some has been a problem; the soles have begun to separate on these, a common experience that prompts many to buy commercial versions.

Right: A great deal of the modern revolution in warfighter gear is based on the experience of outdoor recreation product manufacturers, and much of this crossover has been applied to boots. Originally intended for rock climbers and hikers, these boots hold up exceptionally well in military operations—as long as your chain of command tolerates some flexibility in uniform attire.

Below: Danner boots have long been the choice of soldiers and Marines who spend a lot of time "humping a ruck" over rugged terrain. They are expensive, not entirely uniform, but very comfortable and durable.

Face paint—or "war paint" to some—comes in sticks, tubes, and flat plastic boxes, and in about a half dozen colors, some of which are often tucked into the rucksack.

Below: All soldiers and Marines are trained in the basic arts of camouflage, and some units stress its use more than others.

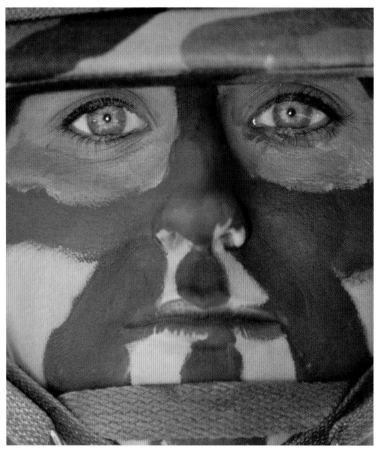

Makeup and Fashion Accessories
War Paint

Soldiers and Marines still get training on how to do their makeup, although it is seldom used on tactical missions. The material comes in sticks, tubes, and plastic cases that look a lot like a woman's compact, but instead of helping you get noticed, war paint is intended to make you invisible. Everybody learns to apply the stuff during training—make sure the ears and neck are covered and keep the stuff out of your eyes.

The army has an approved pattern, but Marines tend to have fun with war paint on the occasions when they have to use it. Whatever the pattern and colors used, the idea is to break up the visual signature of the human face when seen at a distance or in uncertain light.

Snaplinks or Carabiners

The use of snaplinks or carabiners is quite common among tactical personnel. These devices are often attached to the warfighter's LBV or LBE, normally connected to nothing at all. I once asked a young sergeant why he had one on his vest; he replied, "Well, I don't really use it for any-thing—it looks cool."

Aside from the cool-guy fashion factor, the devices really do get used. Some operators attach a single-point sling to the link; others hang their fastrope gloves and other gear on them. For thirty-round magazines with pull tabs attached, snaplinks are one place to store the empties (although a drop pouch is quicker and putting them in your shirt is quicker yet). Originally, the snaplink was necessary for making a "Swiss seat" when rappelling, but since operators do not do much rappelling these days, carabiners are mostly used to secure an M4.

Special Forces, Specialized Gear
Navy SEAL Gear

U.S. Navy SEALs have a mandate to be prepared to execute a very wide variety of missions on very short notice—covert, long-term reconnaissance deep within enemy-controlled territory; ship and oil platform takedowns; direct-action assaults on urban targets; security missions; and many other assign-ments. These can be in jungle, maritime, urban, desert, or arctic environments and climactic condi-tions that range from subzero to near boiling point.

To be ready for such assignments, each member of a SEAL team is assigned a large locker or cage that is about eight feet square, in which all his gear is properly stowed. The locker will contain his dress uniform, ready for inspec-tion; at least one set of BDUs, also for inspection; then several sets of BDUs that are not ready for inspection at all, but are faded, worn, and possi-bly patched and are used only while training. In fact, the locker will normally contain a variety of BDUs that may be selected for the specific mis-sion. Besides the old six-color desert pattern, SEALs may use a maritime digital pattern, solid tan, or desert tiger stripes.

Top: Face paint's use in jungle terrain is much more common than in the desert.

Right: Snaplinks (locking or plain) are fashion accessories for the LBV. The snaplink can secure a weapon retention lanyard, empty mags by their pull tabs, or be used for a dozen other applications.

Although less common now than before Operation Iraqi Freedom kicked off, mission-oriented protective posture (MOPP) gear is still part of the battle rattle issued and occasionally used by warfighters. At MOPP Level 4, all protective gear is worn, including mask, overgarments, overboots, and gloves.

The whole army is adjusting to the idea of a lot of Velcro on the combat uniform, with big patches on both shoulders for a combat unit patch on the right and the current unit on the left. The idea of using Velcro was to make it easier to update an individual's uniform. It has done that, and put many small sewing shops near military bases out of business; these shops previously were needed to modify BDUs every time a soldier was promoted or transferred to a new unit.

Depending on the specific team and its global area of responsibility, each SEAL will have a load-out bag containing gear for specific kinds of missions. One bag will have his dive gear, fins, buoyancy compensator, weight belt, fins, mask, compass board, dive knife, and the other gear needed for a subsurface swim into a target.

Another bag will contain gear required to execute desert operations—desert BDUs, boots, rucksack, load-bearing vest or chest rig, hydration system (bladder, canteens, Nalgene bottles, alone or in combination), first-aid kit, fixed-blade knife, combination tool (Leatherman, SOG, Gerber, or other), gloves, cool-guy glasses, and some sort of headgear. While the infantry and everybody else won't leave home without lots of body armor and helmets, SEALs have traditionally worn a baseball cap with a favorite team logo or a floppy patrol hat on their heads for day operations or a black knit watch cap or balaclava for night. When SEALs go into combat, they do it in style. Helmets are being issued now, the MICH type, and often replace the ball caps.

"My preferences for gear include the standard-issue old jungle boots because they seem to work well for any kind of mission, but one guy on my team used to wear black Converse basketball shoes!" said an anonymous SEAL. "We wear modified cammies with pockets sewn to the upper sleeves, and just about everybody wears gloves on any kind of operation. I am partial to the traditional flight glove, but now you will find guys on the teams wearing all kinds of gloves. I liked wearing knee pads but some of the other guys wouldn't use them.

"We're all issued a multi-tool of the Leatherman type, and they get a lot of use, and all of us carry a fixed-blade knife. My first chief used to say that the only thing you'll use a knife for is digging, but I still like them and own many. As the corpsman, I was also the grenadier and therefore had an M203 installed on my M4 carbine; I normally carry twelve to fourteen magazines for the carbine, plus eight 40mm rounds for the M203. Several types of slings are available for the carbine, but my personal preference is for the single-point type—it makes the weapon less prone to hang-ups and easier to keep out of the way when you don't need it. We all carried the SEAL-issued Sig 226 9mm handgun in a drop-leg holster with a minimum of two spare magazines.

"I use several kinds of chest rig—one from BlackHawk that is based on the H-harness design but upgraded, another of the RACK [Ranger assault carrying kit] type. Most of us prefer a baseball cap. The whole kit, water included, weighed between forty and sixty-five pounds."

Green Beret Gear

Members of the U.S. Army's Special Forces (informally known as the Green Berets) have their own traditions for gearing up when launching a mission. What they select is based on the specific mission, and those missions can vary tremendously, from unconventional warfare (UW) that involves training and leading troops from other nations and cultures, to direct-action and strategic-reconnaissance assignments that are similar to those SEAL teams conduct. Of all the possible missions, UW traditionally has resulted in Green Berets using the most unusual gear, and special forces soldiers have a half-century reputation for going native, often to the dismay of their conventional commanders. While fighting the Taliban in Afghanistan during 2002, many members of 3rd Group detachments let

While everybody in the army now wears berets, only the Rangers and special forces (the so-called Green Berets) have distinctive colors. Rangers used to wear black until Army Chief of Staff Shinseki decided that everybody should be special and wear a black beret, too. When you are ACOS, you can do things like that, but at risk of making the entire Ranger community mad; this is not wise. The Rangers lost the black beret but got a tan one instead, here worn by the command sergeant major of the Ranger Training Brigade. 1st Sgt. (or "first shirt") Russell Mann spent a career in special forces while wearing a green beret.

their hair and beards grow, traded helmets and patrol caps for keffiyeh tribal hats, and wore simple canvas magazine-carrying chest rigs instead of the latest RACK or LBV. All these factors helped the teams fit into the local culture—part of their mission—and made them slightly less obvious targets for any enemy forces within range.

Other 3rd Group teams, like ODA-391 and ODA-392, which conducted vehicle patrols with their modified humvees in April 2003, used a pretty conventional set of gear. They wore interceptor body armor, normally without pouches, and Kevlars without covers. Everything they needed was in their vehicles, including water and ammo. Special forces soldiers are among the best at keeping the combat load to a practical level.

CHAPTER THREE

VESTS, PACKS, AND SNIVEL GEAR

T he foundation for the warfighters' load is their load-carrying equipment in one form or another—what Marines call line two or deuce gear, and soldiers call LBE or LBV. At this writing, the M1967 or TA-50 or 762 systems are still very much in the inventory and are worn by large numbers of men and women while stationed in the United States. Overseas tactical deployments, however, normally require people to turn in their old gear and draw vests, body armor, and lots of pouches.

Left: Tactical Tailor calls their big ruck a Malice, for Modified ALICE. It uses somewhat heavier fabric and stitching and is otherwise modified to absorb eighty or more pounds of gear.

This SEAL is using an old-model tactical vest developed by Natick. It still uses the M1967 pistol belt and pouches while adding magazine capacity across the chest. Later designs added a drag strap just behind the neck, but if our hero gets whacked while wearing this rig, his teammates will haul his miserable carcass off the beach by grabbing the yoke.

There is quite a variety of designs for this load-bearing foundation, each with its advocates and detractors. The standard for Rangers (at this writing) is the RACK system, a sort of bib that puts the rifleman's magazines front and center, without much room for anything else, but that allows for good freedom of movement. Many other warfighters use the PALS straps on body armor to attach magazines and other tools of the trade directly to the IBA, while others use garments that go over the IBA. Some use zip-up vests, and others still use variations on the old H-harness.

"I still prefer to use the old H-harness over any of the vests," one soldier says. "It fits easily over body armor, carries everything I need except for water."

This variety of line-two gear has its foundation in the variety of roles and missions performed by warfighters. Some never stray far from a humvee or Bradley, while others walk everywhere. And, within a squad or platoon, members will need to carry different gear based on the role they have been assigned—rifleman, grenadier, aid man, communications, SAW gunner—and have different needs for LBE. Many, but not all, units currently tolerate a surprising degree of personal choice in the platform used and the components hung on that platform.

Some very interesting and popular gear is coming from a small company called Spec-Ops Brand. Started by a hardcore mountain-bike competitor, Spec-Ops makes a very-well-regarded

This page and following: A Navy SEAL squad has been described as eight guys wearing ten different uniforms, and that tradition is based on a mission-based attitude toward clothing and gear. Nearly every member of this group has his gear set up a little differently from the others—but they still observe *some* standards. The first-aid kit is always at the back of the vest or harness, for example, and SEALs (like many U.S. military personnel) identify their gear with the last four digits of their social security number.

vest designed to be used over IBA, a couple of good holsters, and excellent slings and pouches. Spec-Ops has designed several really useful organizers for all the little things that clutter up a ruck. It also came up with a better pouch for first-aid kits, one that is identified by a length of red nylon webbing. The red webbing makes identification fast, day or night, in an emergency.

The Vest System

The advantage of the vest system is the PALS/MOLLE straps, which permit placement of

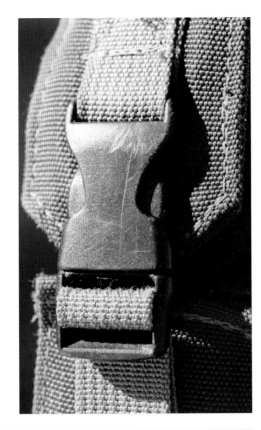

Above: EOD specialists are often assigned to operations with SEALs and have to be capable of dealing with anything that might happen. This one has his vest set up to hold several thirty-round magazines plus some specialized gear required for the EOD mission. The small black object is an IR beacon used to show aircraft overhead where the friendlies are on the ground.

Upper left: Fastex buckles have generally proven to be strong, easy to adjust, and allow rapid access to pouch contents.

Left: Spec-Ops Brand makes two pouches specifically for the individual warfighter's first-aid supplies. A red strip of webbing helps identify the contents. Aid pouches are now placed on the left hip by SOP in many units, although SEALs and others have their own ideas of where to put them.

pouches of different sizes and functions where the user is comfortable with them. The same user can—and many do—set a vest up differently for different missions. A turret gunner in a humvee will often remove some pouches from his or her vest because they get in the way of the M2 or Mk 19, then put the pouches on again when tasked with a foot patrol the next day.

Pouches themselves are available in a tremendous variety of types and colors. Many vendors are producing them, and the competition to come up with something superior has been paying off for warfighters in all the services.

Pouches for thirty-round rifle magazines are nearly universal. Stowage for at least six, and often double that number, are attached to the vest. Each magazine weighs about one pound loaded. Magazines are normally inserted upside down with the projectiles oriented to the right for a right-handed shooter and with a loop, or Magpul, on the bottom of each mag to make extraction from the pouch easier. These mag pouches normally are placed on the lower portion of the vest just above the belt line, although there are variations. Some operators put the pouches farther from the centerline to make it easier to climb a ladder, for example, or to fire from the prone position.

Besides the standard two- and three-M4/M16 magazine versions, you can now get pouches in many forms and sizes for pistol magazines; for smoke grenades, fragment grenades, multiband intra-team radios (MBITRs), the advanced system improvement program (ASIP), which is a SINCGARS variant, and Motorola radios; for pop flares, M2000 IR strobes, flashbangs, and flashlights; for empty mags; for crowd-control batons, oleoresin capsicum (OC) pepper spray, and first-aid supplies. There are other pouches for SAW magazines, M60 belted 7.62mm ammunition, 40mm grenade rounds for the M203 launcher, and shotgun rounds. Then there are the ones for binos and night-vision goggles, plus a few others of various sizes without a dedicated function that accommodate anything that will fit.

You'd think that there would not be much to differentiate the product of one company from another, but warfighters have strong opinions about such things, and many have strong brand loyalty. Construction details have a lot to do with durability and reliability, two features Marines and other warriors consider crucial. Comparing several otherwise identical M4 mag pouches from different vendors will reveal that some are better than others. Cheap knockoffs are coming from China now and selling for much less than those made in the United States.

Top: Two frag grenade pouches plus a small radio pouch installed on Staff Sgt. Tim John's Tactical Tailor plate carrier/RACK.

Above: Some pouch vendors integrate common requirements in a single piece of gear, like this BlackHawk combination five-mag pouch with holders for two M18 smoke grenades.

Individual Soldiers, Individual Configurations

Sgt. Major Glenn is one of several veterans of the 75th Ranger Regiment currently helping stand up one of the new brigade combat teams at Fort Richardson, Alaska. Among his other duties, he is part of a working group composed of all the sergeants-major in his battalion that is selecting gear to be used by members of the brigade. They have a lot to choose from.

The gear we are using today is completely different from what I was issued in the Ranger Regiment in the 1990s. Back then we were still using the LCE as a foundation. I put a SAW pouch on mine and used that for all sorts of things. I always had a Claymore bandolier full of spare M4 magazines, two M67 fragmentation grenades, and a butt pack with the riot-control agent—you could put a lot of weight on one of those things, and mine weighed about fifty pounds.

Rangers in Iraq are currently using two basic configurations, one for riflemen, the other for SAW gunners, and based on a choice between the MOLLE vest and the IBA. . . . We need to use body armor differently on guys doing different missions. For the guy manning a gun on a HMMWV turret and who is exposed to IEDs [improvised explosive devices] and rifle fire, heavier body armor is appropriate. The rifleman who dismounts and patrols on foot needs to be more agile and can't be weighed down with all that side armor.

What a difference the acquisition corps has made in the way we select and acquire equipment now, thanks to the RFI [rapid fielding initiative]! We are getting excellent gear—the army's design for the assault vest, the assault rucksack, and the rest are awesome. Even if we don't like one component of the standard issue—the MOLLE vest, for example—we as a unit can retain the pouches, which are great, and use them with a vest from London Bridge Company, Tactical Tailor, BlackHawk, or another vendor. We like the magazine pouches, and the new first-aid-kit pouch is awesome. The kit comes with these pouches plus ones for flash-bangs, grenades, canteens, SAW ammo packs, and the acquisition system lets us retain these and use them on a different foundation.

I think we are going to go with the modular assault vest (MAV) instead of the MOLLE, but retain the MOLLE as an option for individual soldiers. We will specify a basic setup for things, then give the individual solider the choice of using the MAV, the MOLLE, or putting the pouches on his IBA.

Unlike in the past, we are going to be somewhat tolerant of variations in what soldiers do with the components. Some guys have personal preferences about where they want their magazines, for example. The position of the first-aid kit is the only thing that we currently think will have to be placed in a specific spot, and that will be on the left hip. That way, when a guy gets hit, you can find his kit in the dark by touch alone. Other than that, you can arrange your mag pouches, your grenades, and all the rest, where you want it when you are under fire.

The RACK

Load-carrying chest rigs are always the primary location for ammunition, and the number of mags and their placement will vary with the mission and the individual's preference.

An alternative to the vest is the RACK, adapted for the 75th Ranger Regiment from the chest rig used by Pakistan, Afghanistan, China, and other armies employing the AK series of weapons. Since its adoption, RACK has become a generic term in the U.S. military for *any* chest rig. They offer a good supply of a soldier's most important stuff—ammunition in a very accessible location—

without a lot of frills and extra weight. The chest rig places the load a little higher than the same gear on a vest and makes more use of the centerline portion of the garment since no zipper is required. Variations on the rig are available, but all resemble their humble origins. One team sergeant from a 3rd Special Forces Group team doesn't bother with the expensive high-speed nylon versions; he picked his up in the market of a town in Paktika Province, Afghanistan, for about three dollars and is perfectly happy with it.

Whatever foundation used, the MOLLE concept permits the use of specialized containers for everything that each warfighter needs to carry—holsters, pouches for magazines (pistol or rifle), pouches for radios of many shapes and sizes, knives, grenades (flash-bang, smoke, or fragmentation), crowd-control batons, crowd-control pepper spray, first-aid kits, and survival kits.

"I love my MOLLE gear!" said one soldier. "I like the modular design and the straps—they are

This waterproof bag used by SEALs and others in maritime environments is about the same size as a typical assault pack.

secure, and none of us have to dummy-cord our stuff to keep it from getting loose anymore. The weight distribution seems better and it is more comfortable on long road marches."

Chest rigs are especially popular with the 75th Ranger Regiment, where they are standard issue.

Packs

Monster rucks are not carried on patrols quite so much anymore—they carry too much stuff. Instead, warfighters use assault packs, or three-day rucks, that carry a couple of MREs, ammunition, grenades, batteries, water, and sometimes radios and snivel gear. There are other packs that split the difference between an assault pack and a full-sized ruck, while smaller packs, similar to civilian butt packs, are MOLLE-based and made to wear on the LBV.

Explosive Ordnance Disposal Gear and Pack

Who are the bravest of the brave on the battlefield? The explosive ordnance disposal (EOD) teams have the vote of many military personnel in recognition of their extremely dangerous and important job of clearing paths through minefields, disarming IEDs and booby traps, making safe old and decayed munitions and explosives, and generally being in the riskiest places at the most hazardous times. EOD teams have been attached to SEAL squads on many recent operations and have had to operate at the same high level of performance required of SEAL team members.

As a result of the very specialized mission, EOD personnel carry very specialized gear in a very special pack. That pack is normally made by London Bridge Trading Company, which specializes in the design of specialized tactical nylon products for the most elite U.S. organizations, providing the highest quality at the highest price. London Bridge does not advertise, does not have a catalog, and doesn't really have much of a commercial Web site. The reason for the custom EOD bag is the gear that goes in it. Who else goes to war carrying an X-ray system? The EOD team members have a whole collection of odd little tools and materials—clips, tape, explosives in several forms, wands for detecting trip wire, plastic bottles used for hydraulic charges, and lots more. All of it needs to be accessible in a hurry and none of it really fits in any conventional assault pack.

This BlackHawk bag absorbs a SINCGARS radio, a SATCOM antenna, spare batteries, and the warfighter's personal gear as well. The H250 handset will frequently be seen clipped to rucks and LBVs. It works with nearly all U.S. man-pack military radios, is submersible, and is nearly bulletproof.

Below: This small BlackHawk pack is compartmented to carry mags and other gear in a readily accessible way.

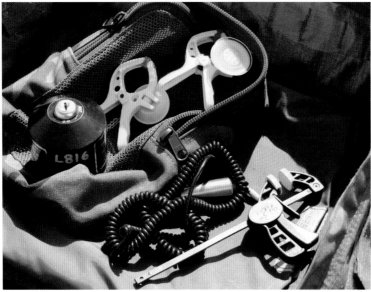

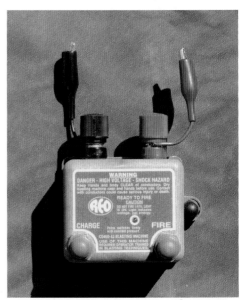

Clockwise, from very top: Navy EOD specialists
seem to use London Bridge rucks exclusively.
Its contents include hydrostatic charges prepped
with time fuse and fuse-lighter, electrical firing
device, X-ray machine and materials, clamps,
and lots more.

Hydration: From Canteens to CamelBaks
Canteens

The one-quart canteen has been part of the American warfighter's issued gear for many decades, and the one in the system today is nearly identical in shape to that used before World War I, the M1910. The old ones were made of aluminum, and today's are plastic with caps designed to work with NBC (nuclear, biological, chemical) protective masks, but they are still worn the same way and in the same place, on the hip, and are otherwise unchanged.

They are carried in a pouch called a canteen cover, whose basic design is also nearly a century old; the ones used today are nearly identical to the ones used in World War I.

Above, left and right: London Bridge provides very specialized gear to very specialized operators in all the U.S. armed forces. Their rucks and packs are extremely well designed and fabricated, with prices considerably higher than rucks designed for more conventional users.

The CamelBak Revolution

Around 1980, an outdoor-recreation company started selling a product designed for bicyclists and other athletes who needed to hydrate. The product was a heavy plastic bladder with a fill cap and a tube. The bladder was carried in a small pouch on the back, a sort of little backpack. The tube terminated in a valve that could be opened by biting on it. When the tube was properly routed and secured, the athlete could easily take a quick drink with a minimum of movement by just grasping the tube and sucking on the valve. This was the first CamelBak, a piece of gear that's now a standard item of issue for a very large proportion of ground-combat personnel.

Some unknown soldier-athlete must have discovered the CamelBak and started using it on road marches. Without doubt, his NCO probably told him to get rid of it and stick with the issue canteen. But soldiers and Marines can be subversive, and whining and insubordination overcame any initial resistance.

Above: Staff Sgt. Morrow has wisely decided to use both a CamelBak hydration system in addition to two standard issue one-quart canteens. This gives him 164 ounces of water available when he's cooking under Fort Benning, Georgia's, summer sun.

Left: Hydration systems come in several sizes and this CamelBak is small enough to be used under a ruck, on top of it, or inside.

Currently, CamelBaks are the primary hydration gear for most army personnel. "We're issuing CamelBaks to each soldier . . . now and contemplating adding a single one-quart canteen on the vest," says Sgt. Maj. Glenn, a veteran of the 75th Ranger Regiment, who is currently helping stand up one of the new brigade combat teams at Fort Richardson, Alaska. BlackHawk makes its own version, the HydraStorm, in a variety of capacities and configurations, and the competition between vendors has produced many subtle improvements to the basic concept. Soldier Systems Command has a knockoff version that is part of the MOLLE system, and some soldiers use it. Many others have the authentic CamelBaks because their parent unit purchased them or because they used their own money to buy them. At up to $200 or so, the CamelBak is a considerable investment for a young E-3 or E-4.

The commercial versions are worth the money to warfighters because they have a variety of virtues not found in the issued gear. The compact little backpack pouch has grown to become

Several manufacturers have combined hydration systems with assault packs, a natural combination. CamelBak specializes in this kind of gear, but BlackHawk has their own line, as do a few other companies.

The Voice of Change

Staff Sgt. Dillard Johnson has deployed twice to Iraq (at this writing) and has participated in some very intense combat operations, one of which resulted in the award of a Silver Star for valor. He has strong opinions about gear and doesn't mind sharing them with anybody, including manufacturers. He has become a leading voice in the discussion about warfighters' gear.

His relationship with the tactical-equipment industry began with a complaint about the hydration system his unit bought under the RFI program. The system was an early HydraStorm from BlackHawk, and the one Johnson got leaked. On return from that deployment, Johnson contacted Tom

O'Sullivan at BlackHawk and unloaded about the gear. To his surprise, that call began a dialogue about the BlackHawk design and changes in the construction of the bladder and drinking tube that made the gear much better.

While all tactical equipment manufacturers seek input from the warfighters who use it, Johnson was impressed with the way his criticism quickly resulted in changes. Soldier input did not have rapid influence before RFI, when the cumbersome process of development, test, contract award, and fielding through the supply system was the only way warfighters got their gear.

a three-day assault pack with capacity for the essentials for a patrol—a belt of SAW or M240 ammunition, several hundred rounds of 5.56mm ammo in stripper clips and bandoliers, smoke and frag grenades, pop flares, GPS, a poncho liner, several field-stripped MREs, and a well-worn copy of *Stuff* magazine at least four months old.

One problem with all of the hydration systems is that the drinking tube, even when insulated, freezes up readily during arctic operations, although that problem hasn't been a major issue for warfighters operating in Iraq and Afghanistan.

Other Options

An alternative to both the CamelBak and the canteen is the Nalgene bottle, normally in one-liter size. Nalgene is a very strong plastic that has been soldier tested and found to be virtually unbreakable. It imparts no taste and cleans easily. Many SEALs prefer it to more conventional hydration solutions, and this preference is growing across the services. Nalgene bottles

are available in a wide-mouth version that makes it easy to add powdered sports-drink packets, dried soup mixes, or snow that will melt on the move.

Many warfighters today don't bother with any of these hydration systems at all; they instead use bottled water purchased in the local economy and keep several cases in the back of their humvees, carrying one or more liter bottles in BDU pockets and throwing away the empties.

"[F]rom what we're hearing from guys in the field now, water is not the problem that it was in the past," explains Sgt. Maj. Glenn. "You usually have a vehicle somewhere close with extra water and ammo."

Snivel Gear

"Pack light, freeze at night" is the unofficial motto of "light fighters" in any service, and it refers to the practice of leaving all your snivel gear back at the forward operating base when you head out on an extended foot patrol. Pain, misery, and

Several varieties of hydration systems – a CamelBak bladder holding 100 ounces, two Nalgene bottles, and BlackHawk's new pouch designed for such bottles. All of these hydration products have their origins in the outdoor recreation industry and have been adapted for use by military units.

hypothermia are all things a warrior is expected to suck up and shut up about, too. Ammunition, batteries, and water are packing-list priorities on combat operations, and rain gear, sleeping bags, and comfort items are at the bottom of the list.

Even so, each warrior is normally issued some excellent gear, and some even get to use it. Much of this gear comes directly from the outdoor-recreation industry, especially the backpacking and mountaineering segment, which has been making products for use in freezing temperatures and rugged terrain for years. As with hydration systems and backpacks, the military's

rain gear, sleeping bags, and thermal-underwear designs are based on products proven in the recreational market.

Gore-Tex Rain Gear

Commanders of tactical units don't postpone operations just because it is raining or snowing— inclement weather sometimes offers advantages, and warriors have always had to be ready to execute their missions under adverse conditions. Modern warfighters have some excellent snivel gear to help them stay comfy when it is cold and wet and duty calls.

It's a bitterly cold late-winter day at Fort Hood, Texas, but PFC Young is toasty warm and dry inside his trusty Gore-Tex jacket.

Until the 1980s, Marines and soldiers were issued waterproof jackets and pants that retained the warrior's perspiration as well as they deflected rain. The result was that the warrior got wet from the inside of the rain gear instead of the outside. These things were also noisy, and nobody really liked them.

Then the army started issuing Gore-Tex jackets and pants in the late 1980s. Gore-Tex is a treated fabric that is waterproof and at the same time permits water vapor to travel from inside the garment to the outside. Perspiration does not accumulate, and the warrior stays dry and comfortable.

My first experience with this gear was about 1990 on an exercise with the army's 7th Infantry Division (Light); Gore-Tex was new to the soldiers and unknown to me at that time. One of the unit's officers with a job in the warm, dry tactical operations center—the tents from which the staff pukes and the commanders run their missions—offered me the use of his on a dark and stormy night. I was quickly converted. When combined with layers of insulation like the fleece shirt and pants often issued with this clothing, you can stay remarkably comfortable in otherwise miserable conditions.

Gore-Tex is still somewhat noisy, though, and that is a tactical issue. When a whole squad is wearing this gear and trying to be stealthy during a mission, the effect is a lot of sound where there ought to be silence.

Sleeping Bags

Avoiding hypothermia has long been a serious issue for ground-combat operations. At places like Twentynine Palms in California's Mojave Desert, nights can be miserably cold, even when the daytime temperatures can be in the eighties and above. The Marine Corps and light fighter army tradition is to suck up the discomfort, shut up about it, and drive on. Both services, however, know that there is a point where warfighters' effectiveness is reduced and they risk becoming casualties before a shot is fired. This lesson has been learned well in training over the past twenty years, and it was demonstrated again during Operation Anaconda in the mountains of Afghanistan.

Marines and soldiers are now issued a modular sleeping-bag system with three components and a stuff sack. The patrol bag alone is fine for moderate nighttime temperatures between thirty and fifty degrees. The heavier

Right and opposite: Recognition panels are another signaling device often found in rucksacks and assault packs. They are one way to mark your position to aircraft overhead—they don't need batteries and don't weigh much and work as long as the sun's up. Many warfighters carry small pieces of the full panel as an emergency communication device, either in a ruck or inside a Kevlar.

Above: Partial contents of one infantryman's ruck—sleeping-bag system (four components), spare uniforms, socks, poncho, poncho liner, and gloves with liners, flashlight, hygiene items, polypro sleep shirt, and Gore-Tex jacket.

The poncho is seldom used as a poncho—it makes a good tarp to cover your ruck when it rains, or a simple shelter if you tie it cunningly to a few strategically placed trees. It will, if you know the trick, turn your ruck into a serviceable raft—for a while, anyway, until enough water leaks in.

intermediate bag is rated from thirty to minus ten degrees as a single bag; putting the patrol and intermediate bags together and enclosing them in the third component, the bivvy cover, is supposed to keep you cozy to minus thirty degrees—if you keep your polypro underwear and socks on.

"The army's lightweight bivvy sack is [a] terrific piece of gear," one soldier says. "I had one going through Ranger school in late October and used it one night during a rainstorm and freezing cold; the bivvy sack kept me warm and

dry, and I actually got some rest—a precious item in Ranger school!"

The sleeping-bag systems aren't very heavy, but they are certainly bulky, and that's a problem for extended ground operations. The army's new huge ruck is designed to accommodate the system and has a zipper that allows access to the bag, normally carried at the bottom of the rucksack. Since half the personnel of a ground-combat unit normally maintains security on operations at night, the unit only needs to carry one bag for every two warfighters.

The Beloved Poncho Liner

One thing you won't find in the outdoor-recreation market is the poncho liner. Whoever invented this simple product deserves a medal. It is light, compact, and provides just the right amount of insulation to keep you from being entirely miserable on a cold night. And when the nighttime temperatures are only down in the fifties and sixties, it is all the snivel gear a warrior could want. Many military personnel use them in place of regular blankets even after they've left the service.

"Everybody loves their poncho liner," the soldier continues. "It is like a baby blanket that you can't get away from an infant! The poncho liner is every soldier's favorite piece of gear, the best thing the army ever came up with."

Poncho liners are typically fifty-six by eighty-six inches (there is some variation) and are designed to be tied to the standard-issue poncho of the same dimensions. When the two are combined they form a fairly good emergency sleeping bag for those chilly nights in the high, snowy mountains of Afghanistan. The normal-issue version uses a sheet of polyester batting covered with a shell of ripstop polyester fabric; some vendors offer them with Thinsulate batting, claiming it offers somewhat superior insulation performance as well as better compaction. Brigade Quartermasters sells a conversion kit that adds a zipper to the edges, which makes the liner a lot less drafty and more like a normal lightweight sleeping bag.

Don't try to take a poncho liner away from its warfighter! Light, soft, and extremely comfy, many military people use them in the barracks or field, and take them back to civilian life as a favorite piece of gear.

CHAPTER FOUR

ARMOR, TOOLS, AND OTHER GEAR

The use of body armor is as old as warfare, and the form of gear a modern soldier wears today resembles what was used thousands of years ago. The issues are the same and the human body is the same. The weight of modern protective systems is quite similar to that of the helmets and chest armor worn by Roman soldiers two thousand years ago. The difference is the materials used. Instead of leather and steel, today's warriors use Kevlar and ceramic plates to protect vital areas.

Then, as now, the use of armor has costs. It is heavy, hot, restricts movement, slows soldiers on the march, and gradually wears them down. Those costs are balanced by a great deal of

Left: Kevlar has been used for body armor for many years and has certainly saved lives. These kevlar vests will stop a 9mm handgun bullet and some artillery fragments but not a rifle projectile fired from normal tactical distances. It is heavy and hot, too, and has been replaced by composite armor plates that cover a much smaller portion of the body.

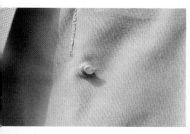

The new body armor combines Kevlar with ceramic plates. This armor is not as heavy or hot, and provides better protection as demonstrated by these two photos of a hit by a small-arms projectile.

Upper right: Entry tools are necessary for breaching doors during urban combat operations, and warfighters now bring along sturdy tools like this one, which is sometimes lashed to a ruck and also carried in specialized carriers. Either way, the lightest of them is heavy and all of them are bulky, but they'll pop a front door in a heartbeat.

Right: What's the heaviest piece of gear you've got in your ruck? After radios and batteries, it's probably your E-tool. The entrenching tool is a little folding shovel that folds into a nice compact package but is tough enough to dig your foxhole or hasty fighting position (although C-4 is much faster and easier).

confidence in the current gear, and the many lives saved by its use. Body armor is required for virtually all personnel conducting tactical operations in combat areas today.

Interceptor Body Armor (IBA)

The standard-issue armor today is officially designated interceptor multi-threat body armor system, or just IBA to the people who use it. IBA has been in production since 1998 and is an evolving system of battlefield technology. It is a modular garment with a Kevlar tactical vest as the foundation. This vest will defeat pistol rounds, small blast fragments from grenades, and similar threats, but cannot by itself defeat high-velocity rifle projectiles. For these kinds of threats, the IBA vest has pockets for inserts, or plates.

These small-arms protective inserts (SAPI) are made of a lightweight but extremely strong composite material, boron carbide, with a reinforcing layer behind. The two basic plates, front and rear, are not very large and protect the vital organs from impacts directed from the front, not the sides.

With both plates installed, IBA weighs about 16.5 pounds; alone, the Kevlar vest weighs about 8.5 pounds. Even with the plates, IBA weighs far less than the 25-pound Kevlar vest in use by Marines and soldiers until fairly recently.

IBA has MOLLE straps attached to both its front and rear, so the garment can perform the same function as a standard LBV—within limits. The MOLLE straps permit installation of pouches for magazines, radios, and grenades, but not much more. Instead of using IBA as a standalone tactical vest, wearers today commonly use an LBV over it. The advantage is that a soldier can shed twenty or thirty pounds of load when appropriate (such as when sleeping on a long patrol), while retaining a basic level of protection against, say, a mortar attack

The Great Body Armor Debate: When Enough Is Enough

During 2004 and 2005, newspapers were full of stories about U.S. Marines and soldiers buying their own body armor because the normal supply system wasn't providing the gear. These stories were followed by others critical of the effectiveness of existing designs and their vulnerability to

impacts at the side of the torso. The stories resulted in political pressure on the armed forces to come up with better protective devices. In 2006, after much hue and cry in the media, additional SAPIs were issued for use on the side of the vest to protect against rifle fire from the wearer's left or right. The IBA system also allows attachment of additional pieces to protect the throat, groin, and shoulders.

Along with the side plates, IBA got what Natick calls an armor protection enhancement system, additional Kevlar panels that attach to the vest to cover the shoulders and groin. The

panels for the shoulders alone, called deltoid extensions, add another five pounds to the armor, restrict movement, hinder airflow behind the vest, and generally make the wearer less agile and more vulnerable to heat stress. Their armor will stop some rounds but not all.

These side plates and supplemental armor do add protection against projectiles, but at the same time the weight and bulk of the plates slow the warriors down, wear them out, and make them less effective fighters. The enemy often wears no body armor at all and is equipped with just a rifle or RPG and a few

After a lot of media attention to injuries to warfighters whose armor failed to protect them, accessory panels for shoulders, groin, neck, and the sides of the torso were added to the basic IBA. *U.S. Army*

M-22 binoculars are issued in two versions. Both are very rugged, have bright and powerful optics, and include a range-finding reticule that permits calculation of distance to far-away objects.

Below: The success of the armor additions is up for debate; some Marines and soldiers won't wear them because of heat retention and weight issues. *U.S. Army*

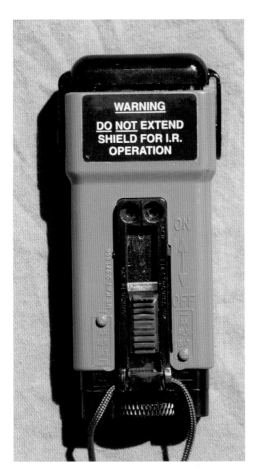

Above: Flex cuffs are used extensively to control prisoners. They are made of heavy plastic and are very strong. When the time comes to release the prisoner, they are cut and discarded.

Left: The emergency strobe is a beacon that can emit either a bright visible flash or an infrared flash every five seconds or so. These are often carried in LBV or rucks by operators. This recognition device has saved lives in combat.

Others swear by the additional armor and credit the new panels for saving lives and limbs.
U.S. Army

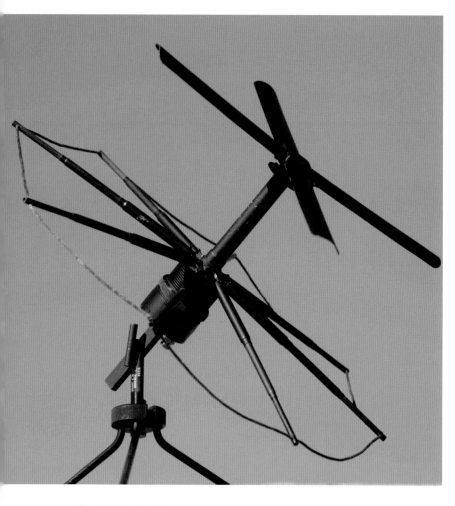

rounds of ammunition; when it comes time for a chase, the enemy soldier has a great tactical advantage: battlefield agility. Over-armored soldiers can be slow-moving targets.

"Every day when we went on an operation, I wore a MICH helmet, eye protection, and full body armor complete with collar, neckpiece, shoulder pieces, and the groin-protector stuffed down my back," says Sgt. Aaron Welch, 10th Mountain Division, who served in Iraq. "A lot of people claim that body armor hinders your ability to move in an emergency, but the policy in my unit was that everybody wore everything all the time, and our experience with it was very good. I chased a guy down while wearing it all and carrying my weapon over a distance of about two hundred meters; I was wearing full kit, he was in shirt, sweat pants, and running shoes, and I caught him."

A full-up IBA system with all its plates and extensions makes plenty of sense for an M2 .50-caliber or Mk 19 gunner standing partially exposed in the turret of a HMMWV or other vehicle where the only thing he or she has to move is a trigger finger and where cooling airflow is present when the vehicle is moving. But soldiers, and especially Marines, are resisting the use of the full-system IBA for foot patrols because of the inherent problems of heat stress and restricted mobility, preferring agility and speed to ballistic protection.

Body armor has become a political issue since 2003, and the army, responding to a public and media outcry over casualties during Operation Iraqi Freedom, determined to issue IBA to all soldiers in theater. The first issue was of the vests alone, without the plates, and involved the cooperation of many companies, which delivered about 100,000 pieces of IBA in just five months. The army alone purchased 300,000 pieces of IBA between January 2003 and July 2004, and the political crisis passed to other matters.

Marines do things a little differently; their body armor system is called OTV, or outer tactical vest. In the rush to get OTVs to Marines in combat, about six thousand vests were found to be substandard during ballistic tests, but they were still superior to the previous Kevlar armor and quite capable of stopping 9mm projectiles and fragmentation threats. The substandard vests were recalled, but the publicity somewhat soured Marines on OTV, and some now resist its use.

Above: With the advent of secure communications via satellite, mission commanders are able to provide situation reports and to call for support no matter where they are. This SATCOM (satellite communications) antenna is one of several used by warfighters conducting foot patrols.

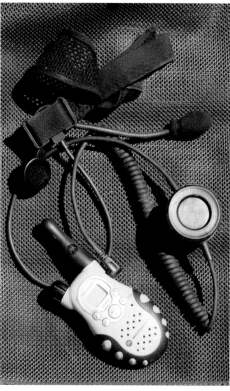

Right: Many units use small commercial radios like these inexpensive Motorolas for urban combat operations. Although they are not at all secure, they are light, reliable, readily available, and can be used with some helmet-mounted headsets.

Knives and Tools

Edged weapons are still carried by most field personnel—military police officers, vehicle crews, infantry members, all the special operators, and all the other people who spend much time outside the wire and outside air-conditioned comfort. They all find a use for one sort of blade or another, and some carry three variations.

Fixed-Blade Knives

Fixed-blade knives are as old as warfare and haven't changed much in recorded history. The materials of a modern fighting knife are different from those of four thousand years ago, but other than that, the weapon still fits the hand the same way and looks essentially identical.

Sergeants will tell young soldiers that the only thing they'll ever need a fighting knife for is digging and looking cool. That is true for nearly all the young troopers, but not for all. I know three men who have killed enemy soldiers the hard way, with cold steel. There are times when you are out of ammunition, have to eliminate a sentry without making noise, or your primary weapon has been knocked away. That's when you have to grab for the weapon of last resort, the blade, and for some it has been a lifesaver. (Killing with a fighting knife is hard, messy work and is not recommended except in extreme situations.)

"I carry a knife as a tool but not a fighting knife," says Sgt. Maj. Glenn, a veteran of the

Left: Some, like the Gerber Silver Trident, seem too expensive and elegant to take into actual combat. Like most weapons, each has its own wicked beauty.

Above: Fixed-blade fighting knives come in many shapes and sizes, from the big M9 bayonet to small Gerbers and SOG blades. The old one is the author's and was attached to his IBA in Vietnam, and he reveres it above all others.

Blackhawk Products Group

Perhaps more than any other individual, Mike Noell has influenced the development of the tactical-products industry. A former SEAL with combat experience in northern Iraq, Noell was one of several operators who saw a need for gear that wasn't being supplied by the usual government channels and who began to produce gear for what was then a tiny, secretive, and isolated market. Since then, his company, BlackHawk Products Group, has grown to be the big dog in the tactical nylon business and includes about a dozen different kinds of products.

The evolution of load-bearing systems had a lot to do with changes in the use of body armor by operators. As the use of armor became standard operating procedure, tactical personnel found that the old M1967-type LBE wasn't really compatible. Two things began to drive what operators needed to wear—new technologies and new missions.

A Navy SEAL has to be able to improvise and modify gear with tape, snaps, grommets, a needle and thread, a sewing machine, or anything else that is available—whatever you need to get it built.

I was a SEAL operating in northern Iraq right at the tail end of the first Gulf War. My team's mission was part of an effort to push the Iraqi forces south, down to the no-fly zone. We were tasked with long-range surveillance and reporting missions, generally lasting a week at a time, and watched many thousands of enemy troops from our over-watch positions. We were typically inserted by helicopter on remote mountaintops and moved to our operational ready point, a spot where we could provide surveillance on a valley. On one of these insertions, the helicopter put us down into a spot that looked safe enough, but once we were on the ground and moved off on our patrol, we realized we were right in the middle of a minefield.

We were, of course, loaded for bear; I was an M60 gunner at the time and loaded down with the weapon and a lot of ammunition in addition to all water, batteries, and other provisions required for a weeklong mission—about 125 pounds in the ruck alone. Just as we were working our way out of this minefield, one of the shoulder straps on my ALICE

pack broke, and as the heavy ruck rolled off my back, it threw me off balance and took me down with it.

When I looked around, I discovered that I was eyeball to eyeball with a "bouncing-betty" antipersonnel mine, the kind that pops up in the air before detonating. If one were tripped, it would fire off all the others, so we were in a bit of a spot. We all stopped movement, of course, and carefully extricated ourselves from the minefield. I made a field-expedient repair on the shoulder strap that allowed me to continue on with the mission, but I resolved then and there to come up with a better ruck strap.

After that deployment I was lucky to be in a command where SEAL gear development was a high priority, and I was able to think about how tactical equipment ought to be designed and manufactured. I left active duty with the navy in October of 1993 and incorporated BlackHawk soon thereafter.

At the time there were small sewing shops near major bases where you could get somebody to do custom sewing for your pack or small-run contract production. Nobody at the time was designing their own products and anticipating the needs of tactical personnel. We started out doing work for local SEALs, but then began making vests and related gear of our own design and having them in stock, ready for same-day delivery.

Building custom gear for my SEAL friends and making sure they had what they needed was very satisfying, but you have to give away a lot when doing custom work; it is not an efficient use of time or materials, and you can't realistically charge for all the time you put into a job. Those first few years were rough, and I had to hock my car a few times to make the payroll or buy materials. Then, while still doing custom sewing, we decided to start doing volume manufacturing to get control of production costs.

Our first product was a bag for explosive-ordnance disposal (EOD) units, a very specialized requirement, and we still serve those units today. Then door-breaching and entry tools became essential gear for SEALs, and we began offering these tools and backpacks to transport them. The need to keep these tools together and ready for deployment inspired the load-out bag, another idea that found a receptive audience.

We didn't have one product that suddenly made us successful. It was a combination of events, personalities, and experience that together changed the way warfighters are equipped. Our products were noticed and recognized as a better system, and word got around the SEAL community. Commanders and the people who are responsible for supplying gear recognized that there was a need for improved products; they'd been doing a great job of equipping the warfighter from the ground up, and they began working with private industry to come up with better gear.

About the same time, law-enforcement special tactical units were going through the same sort of upgrade, and it was logical to start making some of our products in black to accommodate these users. Our attitude was that both military personnel and SWAT cops go in harm's way, and we wanted to build products that would help both communities execute their missions safely and successfully.

The design of tactical load-bearing gear has evolved from the old H-harness and Y-harness into a lot of different styles of LBVs today. These designs are driven by the kind of mission our warfighters are executing and also by the freedom they have today to configure their gear to personal preference. A guy getting in and out of a vehicle all day will want his pistol and pouches configured one

way, while another guy doing extended foot patrols will probably want to set his up differently, using different components.

For those special units that execute the same sort of mission in different parts of the world, a member will have one load-out bag that might be tan in color, and inside that he has all the gear he's going to use in a desert operation. He'll also have a green load-out bag with a complete kit for use in jungle and similar terrain. He is also likely to have a black bag with SWAT-type LBV and tactical gear intended for urban combat. He may also have yet another with a set for cold-weather mountain operations.

Warfighters today are more modular and flexible in what they carry and how they carry it, a big improvement on how it was done in the past. I think warfighter-gear development during the next decade will move toward the integration of individual components.

We've been hearing from the warfighters downrange that they have problems with the bulk of the current layers of gear and with the way the individual things they use fit together. For example, in the past, somebody might come out with a new light or laser for use on a pistol, and it would be a fine product—but it wouldn't fit in any available holster, and no suitable holster would be sold for it for six months or a year. So at BlackHawk, we're working to integrate things like pistol-light development and pistol-holster development, and bring out both at the same time (something we did recently). We're working to make BlackHawk a company that designs and supplies gear with all the other items in mind, starting from the ground up. My mission for the next few years is to integrate and consolidate the development of these components. BlackHawk is now a team of ten different brands, each for a different kind of warfighter-gear requirement. When we look at all this stuff as components of a modular system, we can make the warfighter gear more effective, efficient, lighter, more streamlined, and fully integrated.

75th Ranger Regiment. "But then you hear stories like the one about [someone's] hand-to-hand fight with an insurgent during combat in Mosul that makes you reconsider. He ended up on the ground with the guy when his M4 went black and had to choke [the guy] for quite a while. A fixed-blade knife mounted on his vest, easily accessible, would have been useful, but you'd never think that a battalion command sergeant major would find himself going hand to hand with somebody. I know I have never been in the habit of carrying a fighting knife."

U.S. Navy Mk 3 dive knife used by SEALs.

Below left: "The only thing you'll ever use that big knife for is digging!" Gunny likes to tell his young Marines, and that is mostly true. Once in a while, though, when everything else goes "black" on you, a fixed-blade knife can take an enemy's life and save your own. I have three friends who've killed enemy soldiers with a knife, and none of them enjoyed the process but preferred it to the alternative.

Far right: Folding knives probably get more use than any other edged weapon or tool. Most are now designed for quick one-handed opening and have spring clips for storage on IBA or pants pockets. The fancy ones have cute little accessories that you will probably never need—seat-belt cutter, safety-glass breaker, or explosive priming spike—but they're cool anyway. The good ones are very expensive—these are $100 to $500 each.

But modern blades are useful for other things, too. You can dig holes in a dirt road when you want to emplace an antitank mine, or cut up an MRE box when you need the cardboard for some project. They're pretty good for cutting 550 cord, blasting-time fuse, and "det" cord, and for chopping vegetables. One very practical use for them on the urban battlefield is for getting the attention of the locals who tend to disregard threats with carbines and larger weapons, but who are often impressed with the display of a big knife.

The U.S. Army issues the M9 bayonet, a large and heavy weapon with its own large and heavy scabbard. The two can be used together as a somewhat clumsy but functional wire cutter, but this is seldom done. The M9 tends to be left back in the footlocker instead of carried on patrol. It and similar large knives of this type weigh just less than two pounds.

For those who elect to carry a fixed blade knife at all—a minority—lighter models are available in the exchange, from catalogs, or from places like Ranger Joe's, the legendary soldier's store right outside Fort Benning's main gate. The old Kabar has been popular for about fifty years and hasn't changed in all that time. It is a simple, clean, durable piece of steel with a grip that fits most hands well and a leather scabbard that looks antique next to the modern plastic versions.

Like many Marines and soldiers, Staff Sgt. Dillard Johnson has strong feelings about his choice of blade. "Gerber's LMF II is, in my opinion, the best soldier's knife ever designed," he says. "I have used it as a hammer, used the point on the back to break house glass, auto side-window glass, and windshields, and it cuts very well. The grip is a material that seems to stick to your hand when it gets wet, and the scabbard has a good sharpener built in. The scabbard also is set up to easily attach to the MOLLE straps."

Folding Knives

Folders, as they are called, are popular and useful. Most now have a clip at the back of the grip that helps secure the knife to a pocket or a PALS strap on a vest. They will do most of the same jobs asked of a fixed blade, but are much lighter and more compact. They are not very good for stabbing or digging, but you can cut up a storm with any of them. Folders of good quality are available from $25 to $250 and up, but, in the immortal words of one experienced sergeant, "I never take a knife into the field that I can't afford to lose!"

Building a Better Flashlight

Mike Noell explains how BlackHawk Products Group is working to improve one basic piece of gear: the flashlight.

Flashlights seem to be such simple tools for a warfighter—you turn them on, they make light, you turn them off when you're finished—but this is another device that we are looking at in a fresh way and including in our modular approach to equipping warfighters.

A flashlight can perform several functions, but tactical lights—unlike civilian versions—have to be capable of one-handed function. We found that warfighters are carrying three or four different illumination tools and are trying to consolidate some of the functions of those tools so, instead of four lights a guy carries, maybe we can help him do the same things with just two; that reduces his load and the complexity of his kit. This means the warfighter can rely on one tool to do multiple roles, simplifying his thought process. Giving a light a powerful strobe capability, for example, [that] can be used to confuse and disorient your opponent . . . this is something we've pioneered. When several people on a team use this kind of strobe light, the effect is tremendous, and it gives the team an opportunity to avoid the use of lethal force in some conditions.

Right and below:
Combination or multi-tools are a sort of Swiss army knife on steroids. They work as pliers, wire cutters, saws, screwdrivers, files, and offer a few other common functions. Each component tool is small but often invaluable when, for example, a sniper needs to cut a sapling for his final firing-position hide and nothing else is available to quietly do the job.

Multi-Tools

"Combination tools are the greatest things in a soldier's world," declares one soldier. Virtually all field soldiers and military personnel who don't work in an office own and use a combination tool that looks like a cross between a Swiss army knife and a pair of pliers. The first of these showed up on the civilian market many years ago and was made by the Leatherman Company. Leatherman still makes them, but Gerber and SOG now make very similar versions.

Different warfighters prefer different brands. One soldier says, "I carry a Leatherman, but some units issue the Gerber version. Leathermans have a reputation for being more durable than the Gerbers. The SOG multi-tool is also terrific—the gear design SOG uses gives you more leverage, and they are as durable as the Leatherman."

Staff Sgt. Dillard Johnson has a different opinion. "I used to be a strong believer in Leatherman tools," he says. "But when I got shot

in my left hand and needed to use the tool to repair an antenna so we could call for help, I could not get the Leatherman open—you need two hands for it and I had just one. My gunner gave me his Gerber multi-tool, and you can flip that one open with one hand; with it, I was able to get the wire hooked up, and we had commo again. The new ones now have blasting-cap crimpers and a priming spike for preparing explosives."

Warfighters carry multi-tools where they are quickly accessible because they are used so often to repair weapons sling attachments, to repair MICH helmet night-vision-goggle mount brackets, to cut wire of many kinds, and for many cutting and filing jobs. SOG and other companies produce a version with a dynamite-cap crimper, and other tools have built-in priming spikes to prepare C-4 and dynamite by forming a cap well.

First-Aid Kits

Soldiers have been carrying first-aid kits of some type since World War II, but until recently the standard-issue item was a single compression bandage carried in a small pouch attached to the upper portion of the M1967 harness' left suspender. This is still standard operating procedure in many units using the old gear.

The pressure bandage is adequate for only a fairly small proportion of wounds and injuries, so a whole new system of tools and resources is showing up in the gear carried by modern warriors

Quick Clot

The biggest threat to a wounded warrior is blood loss. It doesn't take very long for someone to bleed out or lose enough blood volume that the heart doesn't have enough fluid to function. Even seemingly minor wounds can lose enough blood

Gerber and SOG make versions with a blasting cap crimper—and, trust me, you don't want to use anything except a proper crimper to attach a time fuse to a blasting cap!

This page and opposite: This tiny survival kit is smaller than a pack of cards but includes a multi-tool, first-aid items, fire-starting materials, compass, fishhooks, and more.

A SEAL's Aid Kit

An aid man on a U.S. Navy SEAL team shares the contents of his first-aid kit and explains how it's carried.

Our kits on the SEAL teams generally include two rolls of Kerlix, some packs of Quick Clot or other clotting agent, a pair of scissors or trauma shears, an Asherman chest seal (developed by a SEAL, HM2 Asherman), one of the new SATs (the self-applied tourniquet), a Chitosan bandage with its own clotting agent, an Ace bandage, plus a standard-issue cravat (a large piece of cloth that is designed for use as a sling, but that is widely used as a scarf commonly called a drive-on rag), and normally an airway, either a J-tube type or pharyngeal or a nasal tube (fitted to the individual carrying the kit).

Each guy on the assault team needs to know exactly where to find the kit on every other guy, so we marked ours with a large black cross on the kit, often along with his blood type. For a while, some teams were putting the kits on the back of the gear to make the magazines more accessible, but the problem with that is, if you get hit, you are going to probably end up on your back sooner or later, with the aid kit underneath your sorry carcass where your buddies can't get at it. I made my guys carry it on the hip or the front.

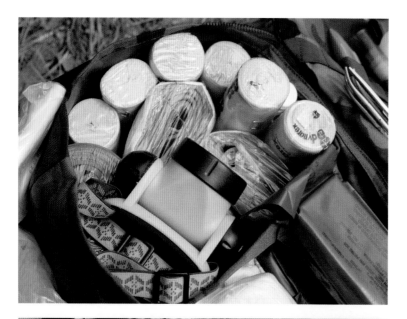

While many soldiers and Marines are trained and certified as combat lifesavers, medics have greater proficiency and carry much more trauma treatment supplies. This Ranger is ready to treat anything from heat stress to broken legs and bullet wounds with supplies from his medic bag.

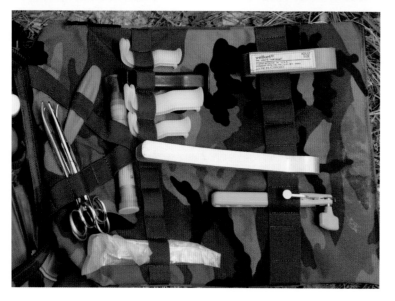

Left, top to bottom: A medic's specialized bag is designed to neatly store dozens of different items—elastic bandages, Asherman blow-out seals for sucking chest wounds, tourniquets to stop bleeding on extremities, IV bags and lines, airways in several sizes, flexible and rigid splints to immobilize broken bones, scalpels and hemostats and other tools for emergency surgery, pressure bandages, and clotting agents to use when a warfighter is bleeding out.

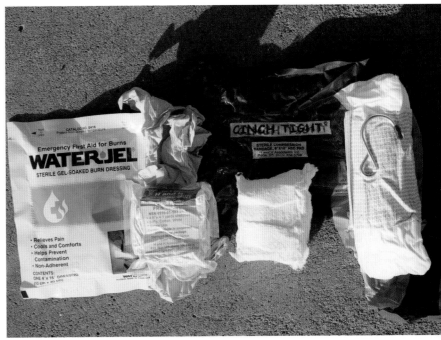

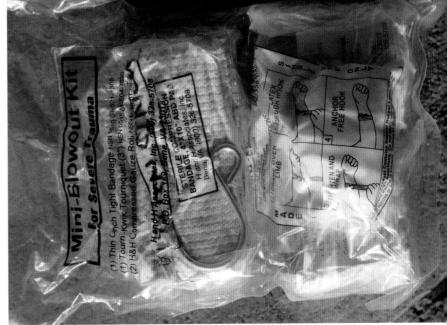

to result in a pretty quick death. Clotting agents applied directly to these wounds accelerate the body's natural clotting process, sealing the wound almost immediately.

Quick Clot is one of several such agents sometimes carried by U.S. warfighters. It comes in two forms, one a powder and the other a thin sponge, and both are often found in aid kits. Other clotting agents are now used as part of bandages carried by medics and in combat-lifesaver bags, and these bandages are sometimes carried by the warfighters themselves.

Cravat

The cravat is a simple piece of thin fabric with many uses. It is big enough to secure gauze (such as Kerlix-brand rolled gauze) or to function as a sling for a broken arm. It can be converted into a tourniquet fairly quickly. It also has nonmedical uses and makes a great scarf, normally called a drive-on rag.

Advanced Tourniquet

All Rangers, SEALs, most Green Berets, and a lot of conventional infantry Marines and soldiers are currently equipped with a new tourniquet that

can be applied with one hand. During a fight, soldiers are trained that the best way to help a wounded teammate is to kill the enemy first, then attend to injuries second. The one-handed tourniquet means that the injured person can deal with a wound immediately instead of having to wait for help from other members of the team. These new tourniquets have been very effective at controlling high-volume blood loss and are credited with saving many lives.

Advanced trauma treatment supplies have become common in the individual aid kits of operators in the "box," including these kits for burns and wounds. They will all fit into one of Spec-Ops Brand's special aid pouches.

CHAPTER FIVE

WEAPONS

A major component of the warfighter's load is his or her weapon system. Americans carry M4 carbines in several variations, M16A2 and A-4 rifles, M249 SAWs, M240 medium machine guns, M24 and M21 sniper rifles, M9 and Sig 226 handguns, plus occasionally more exotic firearms in the special-operations community, such as the Heckler & Koch MP5. As with all the rest of the warfighter's tools of the trade, weapons are customized, modified, dressed up, and accessorized with a degree of flexibility that is new to the armed forces. The number of accessories and the camouflage paint on a warrior's weapon are also a major part of the cool-guy factor.

Left: M24 sniper rifles ready to engage targets on Fort Benning's Mertens Range. The M24 will put a bullet in a man's chest at half a mile, if he gives you the chance and you can read the wind and adjust the Leopold Mk 3 scope and can calculate the distance to the target.

The M16 rifle has evolved from a rather shaky beginning to a respected, reliable weapon that is fairly tolerant of adverse conditions, even full immersion in water.

M240 machine gun. This weapon is heavy but far more reliable and effective than the M249 SAW. It fires the 7.62mm NATO round and is effective against area targets to about 1,100 meters.

Long Guns: Slings, Sights, and Lights
M4 Carbine

It's hard to believe that the American warrior is still using the same basic rifle more than forty years after its initial issue to the U.S. Army and fifty years after it was designed, but today's M4 carbine and M16 rifle are only slightly modified versions of the original. Of the two, the more compact M4 is more commonly used by most military personnel. It's the standard-issue weapon for army personnel, SEALs, Green Berets, and other special-operations personnel. The Marine Corps still relies on the M16 rifle to a large degree.

Both use virtually identical lower receivers, but the M4 carbine's stock is collapsible and its barrel is shorter. The shorter barrel does not allow complete propellant burning, and consequently, the ballistics of carbine-fired projectiles are slightly inferior to those of the M16, one probable reason the Marines prefer that rifle.

A Clean Weapon is a Happy Weapon

Staff Sgt. Dillard Johnson, who served in Iraq, recommends his favorite weapons-cleaning kit.

Gerber and Otis came up with a neat weapons-cleaning kit that combines the compact pull-through design that Otis has made for years with a Gerber multi-tool and a flashlight. The kit includes all the accessories needed to clean anything from carbines and pistols to twelve-gauge shotguns. My unit bought ours on the local market and issued one to every squad leader. It is carried on the MOLLE gear so it doesn't get lost in an ammo can back in a vehicle, as used to happen with the old segmented-rod kit.

An M4 carbine tricked out with an M203 grenade launcher, AN/PEQ-4 laser aiming module, and ACOG scope; the sight is only four power but has proved to extend the effective range of the weapon to 600 meters. Without a scope, the M4 or M16's normal maximum effective range is only 300 meters (U.S. Army) or 500 meters (Marine Corps)—depending on the shooter.

The M1913 rail was developed at the U.S. Army's Picatinny Arsenal and, to the probable surprise of its designers, has revolutionized the way long guns are now used.

The M16 originally had a full-auto firing capability, but U.S. and enemy forces soon discovered that only the first couple of rounds from such a burst went anywhere near the point of aim, and the rest went harmlessly into the air. That resulted in the M16A2 version, fielded in the 1980s, with only single-shot and three-shot-burst capability. The M16A2, now slightly modified and designated the M16A4, is currently the primary weapon for Marine riflemen.

Since the introduction of the SOPMOD M4 in 1998, the carbine has been heavily customized with the addition of accessories, most designed to attach to the M1913 rail (commonly called the Picatinny) that is incorporated in the upper receiver and that may also be used to replace the forward handgrip assembly. On many M4s you will find a PEQ-2 (pronounced

About the same weight and shape as a rifle's normal fore-end grip, the M1913's rails permit the mounting of accessory sights, lights, and grips. A large proportion of weapons used by SOF operators have been converted to the Picatinny rail system.

Left and opposite bottom: SEALs do a *lot* of shooting in the weeks before deployment and conduct many sorts of drills, individually and on line. One of these is called *rattle battle* and involves applying sustained suppressive fire on an enemy while attacking or withdrawing in bounds. The training involves shooting vast quantities of 5.56mm ammo from M4 carbines and the Mk 46 (as shown, a variant of the M249 SAW) plus a considerable amount of rolling around in the sand.

An M203 grenade launcher with a bandolier of "golden eggs"—high-explosive 40mm rounds.

The M203 at Work

Staff Sgt. Dillard Johnson describes using an M203 grenade launcher in combat in Iraq.

I was chasing three insurgents who set off an IED.... They fired at me, and I took two rounds on my vest. Two of the insurgents were in a boat, the other [was] where he had fallen when I shot him during the chase. My M4 was momentarily inoperative and all I had left was the M203, so I fired it at one of the guys; the projectile went through the floor of the boat and detonated underneath, killing both and spraying me with shrapnel and a lot of other things.

This was the second time I have blown myself up with an M203—the first time was when I used one to blow open a door. Unfortunately, on the other side of the door was a large supply of RPG rounds and other explosives, some of which detonated. The building was leveled, and me with it. When the guys got all the bricks off me, I thought for a minute that those 40mm HE rounds were more powerful than expected.

"peck-two") target pointer and illuminator, a more-or-less standard visible-light flashlight, a fore-end vertical grip, an M203 grenade launcher, the advanced combat optical gunsight (ACOG) for the rifle, another sight for the grenade launcher, and often a folding iron backup sight. Other sights and accessories are used, too, especially the M68 for CQB, and now sound suppressors.

The PEQ-2 has two light sources, both invisible to the unaided eye. One is a laser beam that indicates the weapon's point of impact at close ranges, the other is a broad beam that functions like a flashlight to illuminate a general area. Both require the use of night-vision devices, normally the PVS-14 often seen installed on warfighters' helmets. PEQ-2s are in very wide use and have allowed U.S. forces to be very effective during night operations in urban areas.

ACOG gives a rifleman a compact, tough telescopic sight of four power and a substantially improved probability of kill (PK) at longer ranges. With the standard iron sights used on the M4 and M16, soldiers are trained to hit targets out to 300 meters, Marines out to 500 meters. The long-engagement ranges frequently encountered in Iraq and especially Afghanistan have resulted in a new emphasis on longer-range shooting. Reports from warfighters who have used the ACOG in combat have been very favorable, with kills claimed at ranges out to 800 meters.

An M203 grenade launcher throws 40mm projectiles out to about 350 meters and is a handy little weapon accessory that enables a rifleman to deliver indirect fire against area targets. It is a single-shot device that fires tear-gas, high-explosive, illumination, and smoke rounds.

Weapon Lights

Weapon-mounted lights and lasers weren't needed when engagement ranges were 100 meters and beyond. But now that patrols are operating in dark alleys and raiding buildings in the middle of the night, warfighters often have one or more illumination devices attached to their weapons.

Easily the most common weapon lights are the Surefire lights that attach to the M4 carbine, normally by way of the M1913 rail that is becoming

This SEAL's M4 carbine is about to put the last round from a three-shot burst downrange. It is equipped with an ACOG sight and a laser aiming module. It also has a Surefire light attached to the M1913 Picatinny rail and a pressure switch installed on the vertical fore-end grip. This latter accessory is often called a *gangster grip* for its resemblance to the one on the .45-caliber Thompson submachine gun.

a standard feature of tactical long guns. The systems are all rugged, quite powerful, and have specialized switches intended for tactical use.

The origin of weapons lights goes back to the Maglite, the first of the high-tech illumination products. The Maglite flashlight was first introduced in 1979 and became popular with law-enforcement

Surefire lights are easily the most common type used on weapons by U.S. operators. The fore-end grip light is a favorite with SEALs and other operators with a CQB mission. The light can be controlled for momentary operation with pressure switches on the vertical grip.

Two small LEDs, controlled by another switch on the grip, provide just enough light to move through difficult terrain in the dark.

and military personnel because of its durability, adjustable beam, and high output. With the evolution of special weapons and tactics (SWAT) teams about the same time, somebody came up with a bracket to hold the light on a weapon and then the tail cap was replaced with a pressure switch that could be mounted on the grip or fore end. Maglites are still used widely as common flashlights, often with a red or blue filter to protect the user's night vision. But the market for weapons-mounted lights has been essentially taken over by more specialized companies catering to the tactical customer.

Surefire currently owns this category of gear. The company began producing illumination tools for law enforcement and has emphasized those customers ever since. A Surefire light of one sort or another will be found on the rail of virtually every U.S. Navy SEAL and anybody else in the special-operations community with a CQB mission.

SEAL teams currently modify M4 carbines and M249 SAWs (Mk 48s in navy specifications) by replacing the forward handguard with a M1913 rail system, then adding accessories to the rail. A large proportion of SEALs select a Surefire M910A vertical-foregrip weapon light. It attaches to the underside of the weapon, where it allows improved control of the carbine during firing. Pressure switches on the left and right sides of the grip control the primary light, normally a 125-lumen bulb that is bright enough to clearly illuminate CQB targets. A 225-lumen bulb is optional; this is bright enough to confuse and disorient an adversary, although the penalty for that extra light is shorter battery life.

The M910A has two more bulbs, red light-emitting diodes (LEDs) that can be operated by a third switch at the back of the grip. These LEDs provide a very low level of illumination just bright enough to help an operator navigate a darkened area safely and without impairing night vision.

Pistols and Holsters

Until recently, very few U.S. warriors carried pistols except as a fashion accessory. Some officers carried them, and they were required for members of some crew-served weapons teams who couldn't carry rifles for personal defense. The M1911 .45-caliber Colt automatic pistol and

Night-vision devices (NVDs), or night-vision goggles (NVGs), amplify low existing light sufficiently for normal movement and tactical operations. Most can be used on a weapon—on the Picatinny rail—or on a helmet mount. NVDs have become standard issue for nearly everyone conducting combat operations. As with any battery-powered piece of gear, there are problems but most warfighters consider both NVDs and weapon lights essential tools.

BlackHawk Holsters

Mike Noell and BlackHawk have been making tactical holsters for SOF unit personnel for years. Here Mike describes what he and his company are trying to do to improve this type of warfighter equipment.

Drop-leg nylon holsters have been a part of BlackHawk's product lineup since day one, and handguns have always been an essential part of the tool kit of the guys we supply. But we know that there are some big problems with the use of these tools—retention is one, and getting it back in the holster securely when you are done with it is another. To reholster a pistol with a conventional nylon holster and properly secure it is a two-hands job, and we know that a guy in a real-world fight

may be restraining somebody with one hand while securing the handgun with the other. This drove us nuts.

So we went to work on a better holster, one that was lighter, stronger, that automatically locked the weapon when it was reinserted, but that was lightning-fast to draw when you needed it. We turned that into an injection-molded carbon-fiber holster with a latch we call the Sherpa autolock technology.

then the M9 9mm Beretta were both long derided as ineffective in combat by most of the conventional soldiers and Marines required to carry them. However, they were favored by special-operations personnel, like SEALs, whose missions often included the possibility of very-close-quarters combat.

Today, nearly all combat units are fighting in cities rather than open terrain and often deal with suspected enemy personnel at very close range. Soldiers and Marines are operating much more like SWAT teams than traditional infantry. Engagement ranges have gone from 300 meters five years ago to thirty, and now to three meters—the natural range of the handgun.

Warfighters today are carrying a *lot* of pistols. Most are still using the M9 9mm Beretta, but the trend is toward heavier cartridges with greater

Opposite, top: The handgun has once again become an important military weapon as a result of urban combat operations and frequent close-quarters battles in Iraq. The 9mm M9 Beretta has been in widespread use by the U.S. military since the 1980s.

Opposite, bottom: This is the working end of the M9 service pistol, a tool of the trade for anybody engaged in urban combat, where the motto is, "You get more with a kind word and a gun than with a kind word alone."

Above: The SERPA holster features an ingenious latch that locks the weapon securely until needed but which still allows a one-handed draw.

Left: The M9 is typically carried in a drop-leg holster, such as this BlackHawk SERPA model, with one or more retention devices. A lanyard is often used as an additional retention device.

stopping power; .40 caliber and .45 caliber are current favorites. When you need to shoot somebody with a pistol, you want him to stay shot; that wasn't happening with the 9mm "hardball" round issued to most soldiers and Marines.

The problem with pistols, other than hitting targets with them, is keeping them stowed securely while, at the same time, having easy access to them when needed. Many companies supply holsters that promise to do both. Most of these use ballistic nylon as a basic material, normally with a rigid plastic insert fitted to the particular model of handgun.

The MOLLE system allows you to attach the holster on the upper torso area of your LBV, easily within reach. Soldiers who spend most of their duty day in a vehicle, sitting down, will want to mount the holster on their chests, where they can get at it quickly, rather than on their hip, where it is jammed against the door.

Dismounted patrol personnel, guards, and anybody else who spends most of his or her time standing up currently favor drop-leg configurations that resemble the way Wild West gunfighters actually carried their pistols, with the holster on the thigh rather than on the hip.

The Pistol and Holster in Combat

Staff Sgt. Dillard Johnson relates the experiences he had carrying his pistol and holster during Operation Iraqi Freedom.

I carried a BlackHawk Special Ops holster and lanyard, and the combination worked well for me. The holster secures the pistol three ways, including a flap that protects it when you are crawling around on the ground, although other people liked holsters that exposed the pistol more. Mine has been through a few IED explosions and is missing a few chunks here and there, but it got through the mission with no problems. I tried the new BlackHawk model with the one-button release, and a lot of guys are buying it because it fits easily on your LBV or IBA, but I still prefer the Special Ops model for its security and ability to keep the pistol clean.

The Crimson Trace laser grips had a huge impact on the effectiveness of our handguns. Some Iraqi men just don't take you seriously until you pull your pistol and put that laser dot on his chest; then he realizes you mean business, and he stops arguing and starts smiling, puts his hands

up, and walks away. That is a phenomenal piece of gear that has saved many Iraqi and American lives. Mine fell out of my humvee while we were moving and was dragged along by its lanyard for a while before I discovered what happened. The grip was broken in three or four places, and I was distraught at the prospect of it not working, but it still was functioning when I turned it on.

Later on, while conducting an island-clearing operation, the pistol was dropped and fell into the water while I was climbing a bank; I heard a splash and knew immediately what happened and so did my squad leader, who started laughing at me. I fished the pistol up out of the water by the lanyard, kicking myself for not having any of the three retention devices secured, but the handgun and its laser sights still worked perfectly.

It is very important that we get the word out about [using] these retention lanyards because the good ones are saving soldiers' lives.

The SR25 sniper rifle—with detachable suppressor—may replace the M24, but not if the traditional bolt gun community has much to say about it. The rifle is accurate, moderately quiet, and has the capability to get off a second shot quickly, but many doubt its reliability.

Suppressors

The sound suppressor, a previously exotic weapon accessory, is now frequently installed on M4s and M24 sniper rifles. Often incorrectly called silencers, these devices reduce the sound signature of firearms, but certainly don't make them completely silent. Often called cans because of their shape, these suppressors are carefully designed tubes with a series of baffles inside that capture propellant gases and release them more slowly than normal. This slow release nearly eliminates the sound created by the propellant gases, but does nothing for the sonic boom created by the projectile as it moves downrange at velocities well above the speed of sound.

One weapon that can be effectively silenced is the Heckler & Koch MP5 9mm submachine gun used for years by SEALs and other SOF units. The MP-5, when used with subsonic ammunition and a suppressor, is a delightful weapon to fire—it is easily controlled and the only audible sounds come from the impact of the bullets on the target and the sound of the bolt driving fresh rounds into the chamber.

Cans have an obvious tactical function—keeping an enemy from using sound to locate the source of incoming fire. They reduce muzzle flash, recoil, and keep the propellant gases from kicking up quite so much dust, firing signatures that can give away your position. They are also used for hearing protection. Many operators are conducting urban combat missions, often inside buildings, and the noise of weapon discharges indoors is even more damaging than those outside. Suppressors lower the intensity of confined discharges, preserving hearing.

Ammo Load and Pistols: One Soldier's Experience

Sgt. Welch serves with the 10th Mountain Division. Here he takes a break from U.S. Army Sniper School training to describe his sidearm use in Iraq.

If I was manning the turret weapon in a HMMWV, my M9 pistol holster was mounted on the center of my body armor where I could easily reach it, with two spare magazines next to the holster. When conducting foot patrols, I normally carried fourteen magazines for the carbine, a drop pouch on one leg, and two canteen pouches with first-aid supplies in one of them and a notebook and writing materials in the other. . . . I never got into a firefight where I needed all those magazines myself, but we only had four vehicles for support and, as a team leader, I had to make sure my guys had ammo.

Some guys use ACOGs and other optics on their M4s, but I shoot Expert with mine, and iron sights, and that's all I used in Iraq. My weapon was as bare as possible, without a sling or other attachment, because I was in and out of my vehicle so often and slings hang up too easily.

I used my pistol far more than my turret weapon or carbine, and it was quite effective. All you need to do is draw the weapon and hold it in front of most Iraqis, and they will stop yelling and start behaving themselves. If you point a .50 cal or M240 or an M4 at them they will just laugh at you—they know you won't pull the trigger. They take the threat of a handgun much more seriously.

The pistol was always secured with a leash or lanyard to prevent it being stolen or lost in the excitement of some moment. I wasn't happy with the holster I used—it was a two-magazine M4 pouch instead of a proper holster, but it was all I could get at the time. Once, while we were under attack, the pistol flew up into my face and broke a front tooth, then fell into my team leader's lap, adding a little more confusion to the event. If it had a lanyard on it then, at least it would not have gotten away from me.

Opposite, top and bottom: Magazine changes are one of several keys to proficiency in battle, a skill SEALs have developed to a minor art form.

M107 .50-caliber Barrett sniper rifle. Intended primarily for use against "point" targets and vehicles at ranges to about a mile, it will punch a hole through a brick wall and through an enemy soldier on the other side, too.

Ammunition

A warfighter's basic load begins with 210 rounds of 5.56mm ball ammunition, which weigh about seven pounds, and goes up from there to as much as 480 rounds, depending on the mission and the unit. (Rangers in particular load up on ammunition.) Every soldier in a patrol will normally carry ammunition for the squad's machine gun, typically at least one 200-round belt of SAW ammo and often more. Additionally, two

60mm mortar rounds will end up in rucksacks or assault packs.

M18 Claymore

Claymores can be used in ambushes and to defend isolated positions under attack by enemy infantry. The Claymore comes as a kit in a bandolier complete with the explosive device, a roll of wire attached to a blasting cap, a testing device, and a hand-operated electrical generator

Ammo makes up a large part of a soldier's load in combat. Here's a SAW drum, a convenient self-feeding load of belted ammunition.

Below: Thirty-round mags don't come with pull tabs, but they should. Most serious warfighters add their own—commercial ones like this Magpul or home-brewed versions made from 550 cord tied in a loop.

(called a clacker for its distinctive sound). Unlike traditional land mines, Claymores can be command detonated, and when used in this controlled mode are considered an individual weapon and not reported as mines. The emplacing unit, however, is still responsible for removing or detonating them, unless control is turned over to a relieving unit.

M67 Fragmentation Grenades

Antipersonnel hand grenades are easy to misuse and are dangerous to friend and foe alike, so many warfighters never carry them in combat. They are thrown like a baseball and once released, the spoon flies off, a spring-loaded firing pin strikes a primer, and a time-delay fuse is ignited that will burn for about six seconds. A small quantity of explosive detonates and scatters bits of segmented wire outward at high velocity. The effective radius of the M67 is fifteen meters or about forty-five feet.

M18 Smoke Grenades

"Smokes" are frequently carried and used for both signaling and screening. They come in several popular colors—red, green, violet, yellow, and

Operation Pretend War

One of the surprising angles in the development of battle rattle is the large market for such equipment among people who have never been in any branch of the military, and who have often had no formal tactical training. One knife manufacturer refers to these clients as veterans of OPW—Operation Pretend War. They, along with traditional veterans, are reenactors and wargamers (often called live wargamers, differentiating them from gamers playing on boards or with miniatures), and they spend huge amounts of money to buy and wear genuine uniforms and assorted battle rattle.

Although American Civil War reenactors have been around for over fifty years, the modern live-wargaming phenomenon seems to have started in Japan in the early 1980s. Although firearms ownership in Japan is severely restricted, realistic imitation firearms are not. For example, there are no requirements to have an orange barrel tip as in the United States. The resulting authentic-looking—and expensive—military weapons are now sold in many nations around the world, with an orange tip added to weapons shipped to or sold in America. The weapons, called "Airsoft," use compressed air to propel 6mm plastic beads at velocities fast enough to sting without causing serious injury (paintball weapons generally raise bigger welts). Airsoft weapons are useful for some specialized kinds of tactical training, but most are sold to the wargamers.

From these weapons has evolved a very realistic game of playing soldier. While reenacting, obviously, recreates a specific battle and is locked into the historical outcome, live wargaming is about the strategies and tactics necessary to win by achieving goals defined by the rules of the specific event. It is also about role-playing, which distinguishes it from most paintball tournaments, which have no need for realistic or period-specific battle rattle.

People who play Airsoft games often purchase all the equipment used by actual military personnel, including M4 carbines and M249 SAWs that cost nearly as much as a genuine firearm. The weapons vary depending on the event's theme, of course; there are World War II, Vietnam, and other period-specific events for wargamers to take part in. Airsoft wargaming is still popular in Japan, where several large, slick magazines portray young Japanese men wearing immaculate gear and businesslike scowls, role-playing U.S. Navy SEALs or U.S. Marine Force Recon personnel. The hobby continues to move beyond its Asian roots, with Airsoft clubs springing up in the UK, Canada, and all across the United States, along with hundreds of Web sites devoted to the topic, all part of a growing market for retailers of battle rattle.

white. The white version is a very highly concentrated smoke that can be used to visually mask a unit under attack, making it difficult for enemy soldiers to accurately engage targets.

Blasting Materials

Combat operations in Afghanistan during 2002 and for a year or so later frequently involved huge caches of enemy munitions that had to be destroyed in place. The approved method for such destruction involved the skills of the combat engineer, a breed of warrior who likes nothing better than working with explosives. The tools of their trade are C-4, a military blasting agent, a time fuse, blasting caps, fuse igniters, and detonation (det) cord. Typical foot patrols at that time loaded every member with a supply of such blasting materials.

M125 Signaling Device

Pop flares and rockets are signaling devices that have been used for hundreds of years on the battlefield. Today's warfighters use two types, one that produces an airburst of fireworks in one of several colors, and another that produces a flare suspended under a small parachute. Both are launched by hand from a simple aluminum tube; just hold the flare vertically, reverse the cap so its firing pin aligns with the primer, hold at arm's length, and strike the cap with your hand. A rocket carries the payload to about three hundred feet before an ejection charge fires. These simple fireworks remain an effective battlefield communication method and are often carried by members of foot- and vehicle-borne patrols.

Above: Even though the Unites States is not a signatory country of the international Mine Ban Treaty, the M18 Claymore conforms with the treaty because it is usually command detonated.

Left: M67 frag grenades have a fatality radius of approximately five meters, or fifteen feet.

Warfighters throw a lot more M18 smoke grenades than M67 frags, and carry them in special pouches or just hung by their spoons on LBVs.

Smoke will not only mark or obscure your position as needed, it marks landing and drop zones, shows wind direction and velocity, and, when combined with radio communications, can verify the identity of a ground force. North Vietnamese troops sometimes tried to lure helicopters into ambushes this way.

A smorgasbord of signaling devices—a pop flare and a smoke grenade rest on a recognition panel.

Below: Just about everything a combat engineer needs to do the job of blowing things up—dynamite, TNT, and the tools to detonate them.

Afterword

Packing for War in Southwest Asia
by Stephen Hilliard

Stephen Hilliard is a former U.S. Army warfighter who served with the 101st Airborne in Afghanistan and Iraq. He is the current director of research and development for ATS Tactical Gear, a vendor of battle rattle.

Comfortable, Light-colored, Loose-fitting Uniform

Whether you wear 5.11s, desert combat uniforms (DCUs), flight suits, or whatever, make sure that they are durable and loose fitting. Make sure you take some warm stuff, too. Depending on your area of operations (AO), the nights will start getting cool sometime in September.

The sleeves of your blouse should probably have pockets on them if you're going to be wearing armor outside the gates. I wear mostly the Royal Robbins 5.11 stuff now. The company's expanded its clothing line for 2005 and offers some great products and fair prices. The 5.11 line is pretty standard gun-guy clothing, which basically means that it is a rugged line of daily wear that looks inconspicuous and nonmilitary to the casual observer.

The Crye Precision combat/field uniform also looks very promising, and its proprietary multicam pattern is extremely effective over a variety of terrain. Crye Precision is also going to offer the field uniform in khaki and olive drab. These might do very well as a nondescript personal security detail (PSD) uniform, but they are much more expensive than the 5.11 stuff.

Gloves

I like the aviator-style gloves that have become popular for tactical work (military pilots have been wearing them since the Vietnam era). They are relatively inexpensive, easy to find (you can get them through the military supply system), and offer good dexterity and protection. They are lightweight and tend to wear out faster than something like a work glove.

The Hatch Operator CQB gloves are also nice. They are more expensive, but have nicer features. I would find what you like and take one pair for every two or three months you'll be deployed.

Helmets and Headgear
MICHs (also called TC-2000s or Advanced Combat Helmets)

I would definitely put the MICH/ACH at the top of my own priority list. If you have to wear a combat helmet for any period of time, this one is probably the best available and will save you from fatigue and headaches. It is also neutrally buoyant. The old Kevlar helmet—the K-pot—would wear you down the longer you had to wear it.

If you can't get your hands on a MICH helmet, then at least get the Oregon Aero BLU (ballistic liner upgrade) kit and the Specialty Defense three-point chinstrap for the K-pot. This upgrade kit takes a couple of minutes to install and basically converts your K-pot suspension over to the same setup as the MICH helmet. Unfortunately, this won't improve the helmet shape or provide the ballistic protection that MICH/ACH has, but it will greatly increase the comfort level.

A Couple of Good Scarves or Shemaghs

You'll find a hundred uses for them, but mostly they keep the sand from going down your shirt during sandstorms and while you're driving or flying around. The army-issued brown cotton scarf will work fine. A shemagh, the traditional Arab desert scarf, purchased on the local economy may help you blend in better with the natives. They can be used as towels, emergency toilet paper, bandages, slings, or a dozen other things.

"Boonie"-Style Hat

Helps keep your face, ears, and neck from getting burned. Also keeps the sun out of your eyes.

Eye Protection
Sand and Sun Goggles

Anything by Oakley is probably the best choice. Although I've heard some bad things about them, I found that in the dry heat the Wiley X SG-1s also worked well and the lenses didn't fog very much. (I usually sweat pretty badly, too.) I liked them because they were much less bulky than a standard set of goggles, but still offered excellent protection from sun, sand, and wind. I also like the Bollé T-800 tactical goggles, but any quality set of goggles that you're comfortable with will do just fine.

At a minimum, the goggles you choose should be well vented and offer the ability to replace scratched or damaged lenses. For protecting and covering the lens, I recommend the cut-off-sock technique over a flap cover. The flap cover only protects the goggles against damage. They allow sand and crud to enter, and the goggles will be useless when you need them. ESS-brand goggles come with a spandex tube that works even better than the time-tested cut-off sock.

Sunglasses

Same deal as the goggles. I like the Oakley XXs. They offer wraparound ballistic protection and, to be honest, they just look really cool. Whatever style you decide on, they should be *ballistic* glasses. It only takes one little tiny shell or bullet fragment to ruin your eyesight forever. All of the Oakley line offers this protection. The Oakleys are a little more expensive than most, but when you consider the ramifications of losing your vision in the middle of combat, they really are worth every penny.

Hearing Protection

Take a set of amplified hearing devices like the Peltor Comtac or Tac-6. I think that amplified hearing devices are great at what they do, but they really shine when the bullets start flying. I

went without when I was there and just used the army-issued orange plugs, but since communication is one of the most important aspects of combat I'd definitely give mine a try if I were going back.

If you're going to be using a team radio on missions or when you're outside the compound, then consider getting the model with the integrated communications package (like the TCI Liberator II headset). It works with your personal radio and offers you amplified hearing protection all in one package.

Knee Pads

I only used one on my right knee, because that's the one I drop to when "taking a knee." I wore both, though, and just kept the left pad pushed down around my ankle. It's there if you need it, but won't aggravate your leg where the straps rub. Until someone invents a comfortable knee pad, the Alta brand with the buckle closure is probably the best. Avoid the issued Bijans knee and elbow pads. They're hot, uncomfortable, expensive, and the kneecap is made of a hard, easily cracked plastic. Several uniform companies are making jackets and trousers with slot pockets for foam padding (toolbox liner works well) already built into the knees and elbows. BDUs can also be fairly easily modified in this manner at home or by your local seamstress or tailor.

Boots and Socks

Take a pair of comfortable, well-broken-in boots. The Wellco TUFFkushion desert boots are awesome. They feel like a set of broken-in boots right out of the box. I've been wearing a pair to work every day for the last year, and they're still going strong. It doesn't really matter which color you get. They will be sand colored by the end of the first week.

I would take a pair of hot-weather-style boots for every two or three months you're going to be over there. A lot of different manufacturers are making "assault boots" that supposedly feel like you're wearing running shoes. You may want to give one of those a try. For cooler weather, just take some thicker socks.

Speaking of socks, for lots of hiking or walking socks—only wool or synthetic will do. Blisterguard and Smartwool brands come to mind. Cotton socks will eat your feet up so much they'll look like raw hamburger meat by the end of the first long movement. Then, after they have eaten up and blistered your feet, the cotton socks themselves will fall apart and become even more useless.

Lip Balm, Sunscreen, Insect Repellent

The air in Iraq and Afghanistan is, um, a little dry. Unless you grew up in the desert of the U.S. Southwest, you *will* need the lip balm.

I don't think I used any of the sunscreen that was included in every single one of the care packages I got, but you never know.

The mosquitoes over there can be pretty bad, depending on your location, and the flies are really, *really* bad no matter where you are. You might want to take some fly strips or poison.

Carabiners/D-rings

Take a handful of the locking and nonlocking styles. They are almost as useful as hundred-mile-an-hour tape or 550 cord. Make sure you get the ones rated for climbing or rappelling and not the crappy, multicolored, key-chain style like the ones found by the checkout at Wal-Mart. That way, you can use them for actual load-bearing applications if needed.

Wristwatch

The Casio G-Shock is an excellent choice. It is a good, inexpensive, durable watch. It has a stopwatch feature, a countdown timer, an alarm, and is waterproof down to 200 meters (not that you'll ever use that feature in Iraq, Afghanistan, or Kuwait). I'm still looking for one of the tan-colored G-Shocks that are rumored to exist, but CDI (chicks dig it—this is *very* important in the soldier systems world) black will do fine.

Chemical Protective Gear

I'd take a chemical protective mask to be on the safe side, but I doubt it will ever come out of the duffel bag. It may be useful if you find yourself using CS tear gas on a regular basis. I know the M40A1 protective mask inside and out, so that's what I use, but whatever you take, I would recommend that it be compatible with military replacement parts, as they are easier to locate in country.

You may want to consider taking or "requisitioning" a chemical-protective suit such as the military-issued JSLIST (joint service lightweight integrated suit technology; commercially referred to as the Saratoga Suit). There are still a lot of chemical weapons unaccounted for, and recent reports suggest that the insurgents in Iraq are trying hard to acquire the weapons of mass destruction allegedly left over from Saddam Hussein's regime.

Lightfighter RAID (Recon Assault Interdict Destroy) Pack

This is a medium-sized assault pack that I designed along with the owner of Lightfighter Tactical, Staff Sgt. Brad Nelson. We developed it based on our own experiences in the army. It is covered from top to bottom in modular PALS webbing that enables it to be used with any of the MOLLE-style pockets currently issued by the U.S. Army and Marine Corps. You may not be doing much, if any, straight infantry stuff, but it will make your life a lot easier for day-to-day living. I lived out of mine for days and weeks at a time, and it never let me down. In addition to being the best assault pack ever made, it is also a great daypack and carry-on bag.

Make sure to take some extra pockets of varying sizes for the exterior. They will allow you to configure it as a larger pack if you need the additional space.

Load-Carrying Equipment

I kept my pouches and pockets attached directly to my body-armor vest and didn't need a separate vest or chest rig. Make sure you try it both ways for long stretches of time before you rule out one method or the other. I didn't realize how uncomfortable the unpadded straps of my chest rig were, even over my armor, until I'd worn a combat load in it for three days straight. That's when I put all my kit directly onto my armor. The Eagle Industries MLCS/RLCS (my personal favorite) or the Paraclete LCS/Assaulter kit both have a variety of pockets, vests, and a deployment bag in which to carry all the pieces and parts. They are expensive ($1,500 to $2,000 for the complete set), but contain enough pouches to create an unlimited number of load-carrying options.

Don't worry about taking too much kit. If nothing else, there will be guys over there who will need items that you have and aren't using that you can barter with.

On my armor I would carry:

- M4 mags (depending on mission and anticipated threat, the number could vary between six and twenty mags): I always carried one or two of these mags on my first line (in pockets or on my trouser belt). We also carried an MRE box full of loaded mags, frags, and smokes in each vehicle. If the shit really hit the fan, you had a stash to grab from. Keep the mags in their cloth bandoliers so that you can grab one and get away from the bullet magnet—I mean, the vehicle.
- Three to six sidearm mags (depending on caliber/magazine capacity).
- 40mm grenades: If you have a 40mm grenade launcher, carry as many high-explosive "golden eggs" as you can. Then have twice that many more where you can get them quickly (such as in the vehicle or an assault pack). These things are devastatingly effective for destroying enemy positions and breaking contact.
- A couple of M67 frag grenades.
- A couple of smokes (the A.L.S. Tactical Coverage Pocket Smokes are a great option in a small package).
- A couple of flash-bang grenades.
- A handful of visible and IR chemiluminescent (chem) lights.
- A three-liter CamelBak or equivalent.
- Small first-aid kit for everyday cuts and boo-boos.
- Small trauma kit: Include an IV and starter kit (optional), Quick Clot, tourniquet, and several blow-out bandages. The Marine Corps-issued individual first-aid kit is a good starting point that you can build on.
- Dump pouch: It's not absolutely necessary, but can be useful for when you need a convenient place to secure different items that are not part of your normal kit. (Items from prisoner searches, demo charges, and empty magazines come to mind.) I like the style made by Eagle Industries and Maxpedition that fold up compactly until it is needed.
- Global Positioning System (GPS): Make sure to play with it a lot before you need it. It is an excellent navigation tool, but if you are not totally confident in its use it can be confusing.
- Compass and map: Once again, make sure

you're confident with these before you need them. You don't need a huge, military-style compass. One of the simple, lightweight hiking versions will do just fine for most situations.

- Day/night signaling devices (such as a nine-volt strobe, a whistle, an orange signal panel, or a mirror). It might be a good idea to keep these on your first line, too.
- Waterproof notepad, pen, and pencil: Always.
- Team radio.
- Multi-tool: I like Gerber multi-tools.
- Small flashlight (such as the Inova Microlight).
- Cigarette lighter: Even if you don't smoke, they are lightweight insurance. A Bic is fine. The Zippos are nearly worthless except to barter with.

It's a lot of stuff, and it gets heavy when you wear it all day, but this kind of work isn't for the weak or faint of heart. You'll get used to it.

The flip side of that is that you want to remain mobile in case you have to move around on your feet. Work very carefully to establish a balance between too much gear and not enough. Use your assault pack as a carryall for bulky, heavy, or extra items, and just leave it in your vehicle where it is still accessible and can be easily retrieved.

Rucksack

I like the MOLLE II large rucksack with the Generation III frame. It is economically priced, comfortable, and durable. I took the issued MOLLE II ruck to Iraq with me, and it never let me down. The MOLLE II large was born from comments that came directly from the field and is basically the next iteration of the original MOLLE design. The Generation III frame is also the latest evolution of the MOLLE design and is much, *much* more durable than the previous variants.

If money is no object, I highly recommend the Kifaru multi-mission ruck (MMR). It is covered from top to bottom in PALS webbing for use with any of the current MOLLE-compatible pockets. The Kifaru MMR also has a huge edge in long-term comfort. It has an internal-frame design and rides extremely well regardless of the amount of weight it carries. The load will be heavy—and it will suck, don't get me wrong—but the Kifaru frames are excellent at properly distributing the weight. You may be limited to what you are allowed to use because of uniformity, but if you are issued MOLLE, then the MOLLE large will work fine.

If you are still issued the ALICE pack, then I highly recommend sending it off to Tactical Tailor to have it strengthened and improved. If you are a PSD or civilian contractor, consider investing in a nondescript, heavy-duty set of luggage. Stay away from all black travel items—they scream "security team." Try a nice paisley set.

If you're doing any low-visibility protection or security work where you can only wear concealed soft armor, you should consider taking a plate carrier. This will allow you to instantly upgrade your armor level to protect against rifle threats by just throwing it on over your soft armor. All plate carriers are about the same, but Tactical Tailor makes a good one at a good price. The Special Operations Technologies (Spec Ops Tech or SO Tech) Callahan vest is also quite versatile. It combines a plate carrier with a removable chest harness. It's pretty neat.

Knives
Pocket Knife

The tactical folders are nice, but even something like a Swiss army knife will work well. You may even find the Swiss army knife to be more useful. If you go with a tactical folder, I've had excellent luck with Benchmade, Spyderco, and Columbia River Knife & Tool (CRKT) knives. They are reasonably priced, hold an edge well, and require minimal maintenance.

Make sure you take a knife sharpener. This may seem obvious, but I could have made a fortune renting out the sharpener I took with me. For a nonserrated knife blade, my favorite sharpeners are the kind you find at Wal-Mart for sharpening kitchen knives. You just pull the blade through the notch a half dozen times, and it will quickly put the edge back.

Fixed-Blade Knife

I would take an M9 bayonet (if you have an M4 or M16). They can be very intimidating when you're not allowed to just shoot people. A lot of the people you will meet are used to having guns shoved in their faces, but a bayonet is almost supernatural. People will acknowledge it. It's not much of a field knife, but it's great for crowd control. (For that matter, I would probably take all the

typical crowd/prisoner control stuff—baton, mace, flex/handcuffs, Taser, and so on.)

"Rambo" Knives

For the weight of a big survival-style knife, you could carry an extra M4 mag or a couple of extra sidearm mags. You're not going to be sneaking up behind sentries or making a survival shelter out of bamboo, so leave the giant knives at home. A small, multipurpose pocketknife will be infinitely more useful and practical.

One exception is Strider Knives' Model MT-10 Sniper. I've found the Sniper to be an excellent compromise between size, strength, and usefulness. It is a mid-sized general-purpose field knife, and while there are other knives in this class, the Sniper is the only one with which I have any real experience. I was given one by Strider Knives to try to destroy, and I failed. It is a tough SOB, and it can be kept on your gear all day long without adding too much weight or bulk.

I also like the Benchmade Nimravus. While it is half the price of the Strider, it is not nearly as tough. If you have to take one of the giant "Rambo" knives with you, leave it in your RAID pack or in your vehicle. (This goes for the bayonet, too.)

Body Armor

I'm going to assume that you'll be wearing some kind of protective armor anytime that you're not asleep or on the can (and sometimes even then!). If you can lay your hands on one, Eagle Industries' CIRAS (combat integrated releasable armor system) vest is a top preference and the vest that I use now. It comes in maritime and land variants, but they both serve basically the same purpose. (I prefer the maritime variant for its streamlined design.)

I would also highly recommend Paraclete's RAV (releasable assault vest) armor. Point Blank's FSBE (full-spectrum battle equipment) armor is another good choice, and it's what I wore in the sandbox during Operation Iraqi Freedom.

Lightfighter Tactical has just introduced the Warhammer vest that looks like it will be the best choice for someone who doesn't need releasable armor. It has six integral mag pockets, internal plate carriers, and is priced very reasonably. Use level IIIA soft-armor panels (or the SPEAR body armor/load carriage system [BALCS] equivalent) and level III or IV hard-armor plates (the issued

SAPI or BALCS plates are probably fine), depending on the known threats in your area of operations. Take extra pockets that you think you might need, so that you can tailor your load to specific threats and missions.

Survival Gear
Medication

If you are on any form of medication, over-the-counter or prescription, you need to take your own stash with you. This includes vitamins and allergy medication. Don't count on the PX to carry your favorite brand of cough drops. I took plenty of Tylenol and Imodium, just in case.

Escape and Evasion (E&E) Kit

This is something that you will probably have to put together yourself, but the guys at Pro Survival Kit Company also make some really good ones. It should include just the essentials you would need to survive on your own for an unknown period of time in a given setting. Meaning, it should be specifically tailored to your environment and mission. Some suggestions are:

• A small supply of high-energy food (MRE, sport bars, and the like)
• A means to collect food locally (such as fishing line, hooks, or snares)
• Cash in local and/or American currency
• Signaling devices (such as a strobe, whistle, or mirror)
• A small medical kit
• A small amount of water or means to collect water (such as purifying tablets or a solar still)
• A solar blanket.

Some neat items I've just heard about are the forward osmosis filtration bags from Hydration Technologies. They can turn muddy, bacteria-ridden swamp water into drinkable water in a few hours with no mixing, pumping, or moving parts.

Some people say a full-blown E&E kit is essential, but, depending on your mission, you may not need a duffel bag full of survival kit. Think *Blackhawk Down* compared to *Bravo Two Zero*—eighteen hours of surviving on your own as opposed to a week of surviving on your own. Your mission and environment will dictate what you need to carry.

I kept one stripped-down MRE, $300 in American currency (small bills, tens and twenties), a small medical kit, a nine-volt IR strobe, an orange lightweight SERE (survival, evasion, resistance, escape) panel, and a lightweight solar blanket (mirrored on one side, brownish-tan on the other) on me at all times. After I stripped down the MRE, I put the other items back into the MRE pouch, resealed it with hundred-mile-an-hour tape, and kept it in one of my cargo pockets.

Since then, I have found out about the regular and large versions of CSM Tactical Gear's fanny packs. They are a great way to carry an E&E kit or other miscellaneous items. The Kifaru E&E pack is also a good choice and, using side-release buckles, can be clipped (or "dock and locked" as Kifaru calls it) to the outside of your pack for quick access and easy removal.

Snivel Gear

The infantry axiom, "Pack light, freeze at night," is as true as it is old. I froze my ass off the first few weeks in country until our comfort items caught up with us.

I would recommend at least a few lightweight, compressible layers that you can take with you if needed. The Arktis Stowaway shirt saved my ass on several nights. It packs down smaller than a baseball and really works well as an intermediate layer of clothing. The Stowaway shirt and the issued Polarfleece watch cap will bottle the heat in enough to let you sleep comfortably during the spring and fall nights in Iraq or Afghanistan. During winter you will need true cold-weather gear at night.

Gore-Tex

Don't worry too much about rain gear in the region, but you may want to consider something along the lines of a lightweight Gore-Tex jacket. When combined with layered clothing it could also be used as your cold-weather jacket. It didn't rain on us much, but when it did it was cold and there was lots of it.

Sleeping Bag

I actually got away with using just a poncho liner the whole time I was in Iraq, but in the winter months you will definitely need something warmer. I like the two-season bags that pack down real small, like the Arktis Halo 3 or the Snugpak Merlin. The Wiggy's bags are really well made and work really well, but don't pack down as small as some similar bags. You can add a waterproof outer bivvy sack to these bags, and they are usually good as long as you are dressed appropriately and the air temperature stays above freezing.

A good sleeping pad is almost as important as the bag. It will provide an insulating cushion of air between you and the ground. You can find these at any good hiking and camping store. If you get the inflatable kind be sure to buy and bring a patch-and-repair kit.

Hammock

The ten-dollar kind, packaged by Brigade Quartermaster, that they sell at military-clothing sales works great. I think it holds five hundred pounds as a hammock and has a dozen different uses (such as a hammock, cast net, or hide site). They are super comfy, pack down real small, and help to keep you cool while you try to sleep. They keep your feet elevated, giving them a much-needed rest. Be wary of using a hammock when it starts getting cold at night, though. It will keep you a little too cool.

Weapons

I'm assuming you'll have an M4 or something similar. Clean your weapon every day. I think that the M4 is an excellent, reliable weapon, but the day you skip weapons maintenance is the day you'll need it most. I cleaned mine every day before anything else and after every time I had to fire it. If you ride on helicopters as much as we did, this becomes especially important. Those birds will find a way to get dirt and grit into every crevice (yours and your weapon's). Riding around in vehicles is just as bad about coating you in dust. Keep a muzzle cap on the end and the dust cover closed when you're not cleaning it or shooting it.

The army-issued cleaning kit is a good start. I would add a bottle of Strike Hold weapons lube. It goes on like any other oil, but then evaporates, leaving a Teflon-like coating that doesn't attract dust or dirt like oil will. The little shaving brushes used to apply shaving cream are also good for brushing off your weapon in the sandy environment.

Obviously, a red-dot sight, a BUIS (back-up iron sight), and a high-output Surefire-style tactical light are musts. I still see the occasional magazine article where an author without any practical experience downplays the effectiveness of the red-dot, collimator-style sights. Iron sights are great and all, and they are necessary for backup purposes, but if you really want to make hits, under stress, at a variety of ranges, under any lighting condition, I believe that a close-combat optic (CCO) is essential. If you can find one, the Trijicon TA01 ACOG is a good choice for longer shooting. The NSN model has a graduated reticule that compensates for bullet drop over different ranges. The reticule is also illuminated for low-light shooting.

If you're able to take PVS-14s or any sort of night-vision devices, then I think your primary weapon should have an IR laser-aiming device. Once again, it is a huge advantage to be able to bear down on your enemy at night without him even knowing he is being targeted. The military models are good yardsticks for performance, but most of the respectable "light and laser" companies, like Surefire and Laser Devices, make IR aiming devices. These can be tough to get, as they are restricted items controlled by the Food and Drug Administration.

While the IR lasers can be tough to find, it is very easy to get an IR filter for your tactical light that will allow you to conduct covert searches inside darkened buildings and under heavy cloud cover, when there isn't enough ambient light for the PVS-14s to be effective.

If I could have taken any weapon over there, it would have been the M4 I carried with the addition of a sound suppressor. If not that, then an M4 chambered for 6.8mm special-purpose cartridge (SPC; as long as there is some ammo available—ha!) and a sound suppressor. Long story short, excessive loud noises are very distracting and disorienting when you're trying to shoot, move, and communicate. Some of that can be mitigated with training, but if you can get a can for your weapon, do it. Once you're out of contact and still alive, you want your hearing to be in good shape, too.

Magazines are the heart of a reliable weapon. Keep them clean and very well maintained at all times. Make sure all your magazines are clean, serviceable, and run well through your weapon. If you're using U.S. government–issue magazines, the enhanced self-leveling follower from Magpul Industries is a good way to increase the reliability and function of the standard magazine. I also like their Ranger Plates, which make it easier to extract the magazine from its pouch and protect the magazine base plate when it is dropped from the mag well while reloading. Both are drop-in parts and require no tools or modification of the magazine. If you can get your hands on them, take some Heckler & Koch M4 mags. With a steel body and a metal follower, they are the bee's knees—very tough.

I would recommend either a Tango Down pistol grip, a VLTOR ModStock (or the Crane NSW stock if you can find or afford one), or both. They allow you to carry a variety of extra batteries on your weapon and improve the cheek-to-stock weld for the M4 carbine. The Tango Down pistol grip also eliminates the pinching effect that is occasionally experienced with the trigger guard. If you've got a fore grip mounted, I like and recommend the Tango Down fore grip. It has a hollowed-out storage compartment for batteries, an extra bolt group, cleaning oil, and so on. There is also a slot that will accept a pressure pad if you use one for your light or laser. Any or all of these would be a good addition.

Magpul Industries has a new pistol grip called the MIAD modular grip. It allows you to configure the grip so that it fits your hand exactly the way you want it to. The grip also has a waterproof storage compartment with different modules to carry just the contents you want (like batteries, bolts, or ammo) without rattle or leaks. It may be worth trying out, especially if you have very large or very small hands.

Slings

I found that while wearing armor a traditional three-point tactical sling just wasn't working well. It was hard to get on and off, and for some reason it didn't really work quite right. The buckles and connections would get caught on the little protuberances all over my armor, and I couldn't always bring it to bear as quickly as I expected. So I just kept my M4 clipped to my armor with a one-inch side-release buckle and some extra webbing. This convenient method kept the carbine on my person and the butt stock in the pocket of my shoulder. I also kept a simple three-point sling on it, so that while not out and about I could still carry it tactically without my armor on. I don't do it that way anymore.

Now I have a buckle on my vest or armor and can very quickly switch back and forth between vest/armor mount or three-point sling as the situation dictates. Ashley Burnsed of Blue Force Gear offers a revolutionary new sling called the SOC-C sling that can be used in single point, two point, three point, or directly attached to your armor. It can be switched between these different configurations very quickly and easily. He also offers a contractor pack for PSDs that will modify the sling to work with most NATO and former Warsaw Pact weapons just by changing out the buckles. Plus, the sling can be had in a very cool shade of coyote brown or olive drab webbing. I've just started using the SOC-C sling, and it seems very promising.

Together, Burnsed and I also developed the SOC-C-RVS (releasable vest sling). It was designed to integrate into Eagle Industries' CIRAS vest and still be fully compatible with all of Blue Force Gear's modular buckle adapters. It helps distribute the weight of the weapon without affecting the proper wear of the vest and doesn't interfere with the release of the vest.

If you're a contractor and get stuck with an AK-47, it's not the end of the world. Indeed, some consider them a better choice over the M16/M4 series of weapons. There are plenty of options for good tactical slings, the mounting of CCOs, and other improvements to form and function. The best advice I can give is to try to get one that hasn't been beaten or abused. I've heard good things about rifles made in any of the former Warsaw Pact countries (like Poland, East Germany, and the former Soviet Union), and as long as they aren't worn out, AKs seem to run pretty well in general.

Whatever you wind up with, keep it well maintained and shoot it plenty before you trust your life to it. If you know for a fact that you're getting issued an AK, I would recommend trying to take some of the 75- or 100-round drums along with you. I understand they are difficult to get in country, and they could make all the difference when breaking contact.

Sidearms

If you are issued or allowed a sidearm, I would carry it in a drop-leg-style holster. This kind of holster will allow the weapon to be worn with armor and keeps it on your person even if you aren't wearing your other gear. Ideally, this holster should drop down to just below your belt line. A lot of guys wear these too far down on their leg, just above their knee. This configuration is incorrect and will slow your draw as you contort your body to try to reach your sidearm. It may also make the weapon uncomfortable to wear and allow the holster to slide and flop around on your leg.

Depending on what kind of work you're doing, my favorites are London Bridge Trading Company's NSW holster or the Safariland 6004, but Eagle Industries and BDS Tactical make great holsters, too. I probably like the Safariland 6004 the best, as you can easily and securely reholster with one hand and without looking down at the holster. Because it is made of a thermo-molded plastic called Kydex, it is rigid and will protect the pistol better than a sewn-together nylon holster. For this same reason, though, it can become uncomfortable when worn for long periods or when you're doing a lot of walking. I would also take a belt-style concealment holster just in case.

You will need a thick, sturdy belt for any holster. BDS Tactical's heavy-duty rigger's belt is my favorite, but most of them are basically the same. I would just go with the least expensive from a reliable manufacturer. Make sure it will fit the loops on your trousers, and choose a model that is either double layered or stiffened with a plastic insert so that it won't sag.

If you prefer, you can wear a holster attached directly to your armor; Tactical Tailor and Paraclete make good ones. You can also just use a standard M4 magazine pouch. If you aren't wearing your vest, you will have to have a separate holster on your belt in which to move your pistol.

Miscellaneous
Identification Tags

Have a set of dog tags made up and wear them all day, every day. I would put these at the top of my own list right after the MICH/ACH helmet. If the worst happens, it will make things easier for everybody. Make sure the tags have the correct blood type on them. If you don't know yours, donate some blood to the Red Cross, and they will type your blood for you. In addition, we wrote our blood type on everything we wore, from boots to helmets to T-shirts. The seconds it shaves off of your triage time could save your life. Once again, cheap insurance.

PVS-14 Night-Vision Monocular

I don't know how you will be outfitted, but I would put this item at the top of my own packing list. Its use will give you such a huge advantage at night that you will wonder how you got along without it. Don't forget all the equipment to attach it to your helmet and to wear it as a stand-alone unit.

The compass attachment for the lens is a neat extra. It allows the wearer to instantly get a direction reading without having to lift up the night-observation devices and dig out a compass. It is especially important for land navigation or patrolling at night, but it can also be useful for calling and directing fire on a distant target or observation/surveillance work.

Consider getting a small protective case for it that attaches directly to your vest or assault pack. The PVS-7/14 cases from Supply Captain are great and provide maximum protection with minimal bulk. Blade-Tech Industries also makes a fairly good one, but use Loctite to secure all the screws and mounting hardware before you use it.

Batteries

You may be supplied with these in country, but go ahead and take extras for every item you have that requires them. If you have something that takes an odd battery, like the M68 CCO, then make sure you will be able to resupply. If not, take your own stash.

Hundred-mile-an-hour Tape (or Duct Tape)

This stuff holds the world together. You will never stop finding uses for it. A tip I learned from my dad while hiking and camping was to put a dozen wraps or so around each of my canteens so that I'd always have some on me without having to carry a full roll.

Tie-downs

We used these unfailingly for all of our high-dollar and sensitive items. Just use a little bit of gutted 550 cord (formed by removing the seven inner strands from a length of 550 cord). This can save you a lot of heartache as some items will be very difficult or impossible to replace in theater. I've seen several laser-aiming devices or red-dot sights that would have been damaged or lost if they hadn't been dangling off their weapons by their tie-downs. Use no more 550 cord than is needed to tie the item down or you could create a snag hazard.

I'd take a couple hundred feet of 550 cord and a bag of heavy-duty zip ties to be used for all kinds of field repairs and tie-downs. There are other uses for 550 cord, too. It can be used to replace bootlaces, hang heavy items, and the inner strands can even be used for heavy-duty sewing and emergency sutures.

Entertainment

You won't be busy every second, and it's nice to have something—books, a Game Boy, a CD/DVD player, pictures from home—to pass the time.

Digital Camera

You will see things that defy description and live through things that will be a blur after time has gone by. I wouldn't suggest snapping away in the middle of a drama, but it will be nice to have a record of your experience. Take plenty of memory or memory sticks.

Glossary

ALICE: all-purpose lightweight individual carrying equipment, a rucksack and load-bearing system introduced in 1974 and still in common issue

Battle rattle: A slang expression for all the gear worn by modern tactical personnel; the expression comes from the little noises made as magazines and other equipment knock against each other during movement.

COTS: Commercial off the shelf—selecting existing products for military use rather than reinventing the wheel (or rucksack or sleeping bag).

CQB: close-quarters battle

Deuce gear: A Marine Corps term for the M1967 gear, also known as 782 gear or line-two gear. The name is derived from the table of allowances authorizing the Marine his or her individual equipment.

Dummy cord: The stuff that ties the whole U.S. Army and Marine Corps together—originally parachute suspension line, a cord with seven strands covered with a sleeve of synthetic material. Also known as 550 cord.

FPLIF rucksack: field pack large internal frame rucksack

Geardo: a person who spends half their monthly income on gear

Gear queer: *see* geardo

GPS: Global Positioning System

Gucci gear: expensive gear that looks very cool and high speed

High speed: high tech

Hundred-mile-an-hour tape: the military version of duct tape

IBA: interceptor body armor

IIFS: individual integrated fighting system

IMPAC: The international merchant purchase authorization card, a credit card system used by the U.S. military to make small purchases.

LBE: load-bearing equipment, normally referring to the M1967 assembly of pistol belt, suspenders, magazine pouches, canteens, and other items

LBV: load-bearing vest

Line-one gear: clothing normally worn at all times—boots, socks, underwear, BDUs, hat or helmet

Line-two gear: combat or fighting load—LBV or equivalent, weapon(s), ammunition, water, first-aid kit, body armor

Line-three gear: a rucksack containing the logistics package or sustainment load, including spare ammo, food, extra water, and comfort items

MARPAT: Marine disruptive pattern; a camouflage-patterned uniform patented by the Marine Corps in 2002

MOLLE: modular lightweight load-carrying equipment (pronounced "molly"), a system of interconnected components first fielded in 1988

Natick Soldier Systems Center: the U.S. Army and Marine Corps' research facility for gear

Nerf ruck: A ruck that appears to be heavily loaded but that actually weighs very little, because of the use of bulky objects like pillows; an honor-code violation at places like the special forces qualification course.

PALS: pouch attachment ladder system

RACK: The Ranger assault carrying kit (RACK) was designed for the 75th Infantry Ranger Regiment. It combines the simplicity of a chest rig with the modularity of PALS webbing. This type of load-carrying rig is well suited for mounted and heliborne operations.

RFI: Rapid funding initiative, an army program executive officer soldier (PEO-Soldier) initiative to field advanced soldier systems items prior to deployment to those actually going into the fight.

SAPI: small arms protective insert

Shemagh: traditional Arab desert scarf, worn in several styles and known by several names, including *keffiyeh*, which is often associated with Palestinians

SOCOM: Special Operations Command

SOF: special-operations forces

TA-50: another common term for LBE

Woobie: Nickname for the beloved poncho liner; the term comes from the 1983 movie *Mr. Mom*, in which the lead character's son carries around a smelly old security blanket called Woobie.

Resources

BlackHawk Products Group
4850 Brookside Ct.
Norfolk, VA 23502
Phone: 757-436-3101
Orders: 800-694-5263
Fax: 757-436-3088 or 888-830-2013
Sales Support Division: sales@blackhawk.com
Government Sales Division: gs@blackhawk.com
Law Enforcement Sales Division: le@blackhawk.com
International Sales Division: intlsales@blackhawk.com
BlackHawk Authorized Dealer Sales Division: BAD@blackhawk.com
Customer Service: cs@blackhawk.com

Brigade Quartermasters
P.O. Box 100001
1025 Cobb International Dr. NW, Ste. 100
Kennesaw, GA 30156-9217
Catalog Orders: 1-800-338-4327 or 770-428-1234
Customer Service: 1-800-228-7344 or 770-428-1234
Retail Store: 1-888-428-6870 or 770-428-6870

Eye Safety Systems, Inc. (ESS)
P.O. Box 1017
Sun Valley, ID 83353
Phone: 877-726-4072 or 208-726-4072
Fax: 208-726-4563
E-mail: ess@essgoggles.com
Web: www.essgoggles.com

Kirfaru International
4894 VanGordon St.
Wheat Ridge, CO 80033
Phone: 1-800-222-6139 or 303-278-9155
Web: www.kifaru.net

Lightfighter Tactical
15858 Fort Campbell Blvd.
Oak Grove, KY 42262
Phone: 270-439-0302
E-mail: military@lightfighter.com

Practical Tactical
20280 N. 59th Ave., PMB 115-432
Glendale, AZ 85308
Phone: 602-402-7385
Fax: 623-487-8945
E-mail: info@practicaltactical.net

Spec-Ops Brand

Best Made Designs, LLC
1601 W. 15th Street
Monahans, TX 79756
Phone: 432-943-4888 or 866-SPEC-OPS
Fax: 432-943-5565
E-mail: info@specopsbrand.com
Web: www.specopsbrand.com

Tactical Tailor

12715 Pacific Highway South
Lakewood, WA 98499
Phone: 253-984-7854
E-mail: customerservice@tacticaltailor.com

U.S. Cavalry

2855 Centennial Ave.
Radcliff, KY 40160-9000
Phone: 800-777-7172
Fax: 270-352-0266

Index

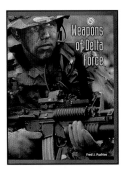

**WEAPONS OF
DELTA FORCE**
ISBN 0-7603-1139-0

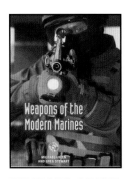

**WEAPONS OF THE
MODERN MARINES**
ISBN 0-7603-1697-X

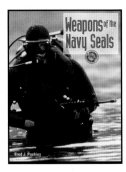

**WEAPONS OF THE
NAVY SEALS**
ISBN 0-7603-1790-9

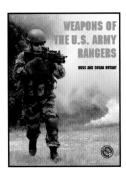

**WEAPONS OF THE
U.S. ARMY RANGERS**
ISBN 0-7603-2112-4

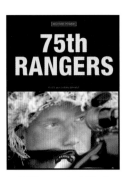

75TH RANGERS
ISBN 0-7603-2111-6

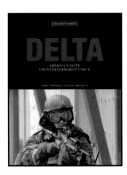

DELTA
ISBN 0-7603-2110-8

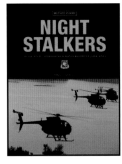

NIGHT STALKERS
ISBN 0-7603-2141-8

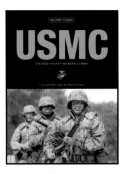

USMC
ISBN 0-7603-2532-4

U.S. NAVY SEALS
ISBN 0-7603-2413-1